How to Keep Your Job in a Tough Competitive Market

101 Strategies You Can Use Today

How to Keep Your Job in a Tough Competitive Market

101 Strategies You Can Use Today

Michael J. Kitson, MBA and Bob Calandra

BUSINESS
Avon, Massachusetts

Published by Adams Business, and imprint of Adams Media,
a division of F+W Media, Inc.
57 Littlefield Street, Avon, MA 02322. U.S.A.
www.adamsmedia.com

ISBN-10: 1-60550-651-6
ISBN-13: 978-1-60550-651-7

Printed in the United States of America.

J I H G F E D C B A

Library of Congress Cataloging-in-Publication Data
is available from the publisher.

This publication is designed to provide accurate and authoritative information with regard to the subject matter covered. It is sold with the understanding that the publisher is not engaged in rendering legal, accounting,
or other professional advice. If legal advice or other expert assistance is
required, the services of a competent professional person should be
sought.
—From a Declaration of Principles jointly adopted by a Committee of
the American Bar Association and a Committee of Publishers and
Associations

Many of the designations used by manufacturers and sellers to distinguish
their product are claimed as trademarks. Where those designations appear
in this book and Adams Media was aware of a trademark claim, the designations have been printed with initial capital letters.

This book is available at quantity discounts for bulk purchases.
For information, please call 1-800-289-0963.

Contents

Part II: Keep Your Job by Helping Others / 89

Acknowledgments

We'd like to thank the many professionals who lent their expertise to this book:

- ✔ James Allen—Vice president of Booz Allen Hamilton, a consulting and management firm
- ✔ Jennifer Berman—Attorney and practice leader for capitol services, the Human Capitol Advisory Group for CBIZ, Chicago
- ✔ Philip Berry—Managing principal of Berry Block and Bernstein, LLC
- ✔ Mary Crane—President of Mary Crane & Associates
- ✔ Joseph Fenico—Human Resource Professional
- ✔ Joseph Gassman—Business Project Director
- ✔ Philip Haynes—Managing Director of AllianceQ
- ✔ Wendy Kaufman—Trainer and executive coach for Benchmark Communications, Inc.
- ✔ Jeff Kaye—President and CEO of Kaye/Bassman
- ✔ Fran Landolf—Executive coach and business consultant

✔ Billy Lowe—Celebrity hairstylist

✔ Mickey Matthews—North America vice president of Stanton Chase

✔ Ross Mayfield—Cofounder, chairman, and president of Socialtext

✔ Emmy Miller—President of Liberty Business Strategies, LTD

✔ Jeanine Tanner O'Donnell—Career strategist and workplace consultant

✔ William P. Potsic, MD, MMM—Vice chairman for Clinical Affairs Department of Surgery, The Children's Hospital of Philadelphia

✔ Lisa Quast—President, Career Woman, Inc.

✔ Marlene Prost—Consultant

✔ Roy A. Roper—President, Roper Consulting Group

✔ Rob Steward—Vice president of sales for LatPro Public Relations, an online employment resource for Hispanic and bilingual professionals

Introduction

By reading this book, you will have taken the first step to keeping your job. You are aware, unlike many of your peers, that your job, along with your financial security, can disappear overnight. At no time since the Great Depression has the job market been as uncertain or volatile as it is today.

Too many people are still stuck in the romance of a bygone era when employees spent a lifetime faithfully performing their duties for the same company. Back then people arrived at work each morning not troubled about job security. And they left each evening never considering that their job wouldn't be waiting for them when they showed up in the morning. Their reward at retirement for decades of dedication traditionally was a gold watch, the symbol of a business's thanks for their years of hard work.

Technology has transformed that safe, predictable routine into the rough-and-tumble world of the global economy. Within a few decades, American businesses have progressed from selling their goods locally, regionally, and nationally to competing for markets globally. Businesses have had to react much faster to continuously evolving trends. The marketplace will keep demanding that business be conducted faster, better, cheaper. Staying apace with the global economy will require companies to remain lean while constantly honing their staffs. Anyone who does not measure up to the demands of their job will be let go.

Even in that hectic environment, losing your job rarely happens overnight. Indeed, the signs are almost always present. People sometimes don't recognize the harbingers of pending unemployment. Otherwise savvy, intelligent people simply choose to ignore or react to what they see going on around them. Instead they hope for the best, choosing to believe that everything will be fine in the long run.

That kind of head-in-the-sand approach does not work. You must commit to becoming a smart, proactive employee who quantifies their value to the company in real, hard numbers. *How to Keep Your Job in a Tough Competitive Market* offers 101 tips for staying employed in a slow economy. This book is based on extensive interviews with employment experts from across the country. Those people keeping their jobs, and whom companies will fight to retain, recognize that being at the top of their game is merely a prerequisite, and certainly not a guarantee, to collecting a paycheck. They understand that they must create, manage, and internally market their brand—who they are and what unique talent they offer—as different from everyone else. They realize that a successful career has to be planned, plotted, and adjusted as they head toward their goal. They recognize the benefits of eagerly and graciously helping their colleagues, including finding ways to support their manager. And they willingly pitch in to save a company in trouble by drumming up business and cutting costs and spending.

The people keeping their jobs at a time when everyone around them is losing theirs will do those things not just because it will help them stay employed, but because, in the end, it will also make them better people.

Part I

Create Your Brand and Build Your Career

Every product has a brand. The most popular and financially successful brands, however, are those whose names become synonymous with a particular product. Think about it. When people need a tissue, they ask for a Kleenex. And copying a document is referred to as Xeroxing. And when kids want gelatin, they ask for Jell-O.

As an employee, you want to become your company's Jell-O, especially when the flavor of the day is Unexpected Falling Economy. You want everyone in the company, from the executive above you to the newest intern, to know that you are the person to go to when it comes to particular aspects of your job.

"Brand is different than just talking about what your job is," Philip Berry, managing principal of Berry Block and Bernstein LLC, a New York consulting firm. "You can have five people who are doing the same job. But if an individual is focused on creating their personal brand, then they are identifying the unique ways they contribute to the organization in a way that others don't."

Several ingredients go into creating your brand. The first is patience. It takes time, hard work, and slavish attention to detail to develop a unique brand. But all the effort of developing, cultivating, and marketing your brand is well worth it because your brand, in a down economy, can help save your job in bad times. How? By setting you apart from your coworkers. Your brand tells an employer that you possess a certain value that is different from what every other employee brings to the company, even among a group of people performing the same or similar jobs. Decide what you want your brand to say about you and then get started creating it.

Establishing your brand is important for several reasons, not the least of which is that it provides a solid foundation upon which to construct your career. Building a career is not unlike building most other things. You start by determining your goal. Say you are building a house. You begin with the style of house you want. Then you sketch out a plan that details each section of the final product, including the decorating touches. Once that is accomplished, it's time to lay the foundation, followed by constructing the structure's frame. Then come the walls and roof. Next, it's time to work inside on the plumbing and the electrical. Finally, the drywall goes up, and the flooring goes down. Add some paint and decorations, and the house is finished.

You can follow the same plan for building a career, beginning with what you want to do, and where you want to be when the journey ends. But instead of using wood and nails, and drywall and spackle, the materials you will use to build a career are contacts and conversations.

"Sit down and have a conversation with key people around the organization," says Roy Roper, president of the Delaware-based Roper Consulting Group. "That includes your boss. Explain what you are trying to do, and seek their advice. You are going to learn some things. But people are also going to have the opportunity to learn about you, which gets you some visibility."

Don't limit your conversations to the executives above you, Roper says. Find out who the key people are inside the organization and seek out their counsel. Ask them how they built their careers and what ideas and recommendations they have for you. The goal, Roper says, is to gain the perspective of people who have launched, and are maintaining successful careers.

"In those conversations, I think it is important for you, as the one seeking information and looking to build a career, to be strategic and ask what, if anything, you can do for that person. From a career-building standpoint, that is a smart political move, and it may get you exposure to some of the types of things that could help support building your career."

All right, it's time to forge your brand and pull out the schematics and start building your career.

1. Come in Early and Stay Late

Arriving late to work is never a good idea. But when a business is floundering, sauntering in late or leaving work early makes you stand out as a target for an employer looking to trim payroll. When a company is in trouble, employers notice the little things, like who shows up early and who bolts for the door like an Olympic sprinter at quitting time. To keep your job during a down cycle, reinforce your brand as a hard-working team player who is willing to pitch in any way possible to help the company.

But in tough economic times, just doing your job, no matter how well you do it, is not enough. If you regularly chew through a day's worth of work in six hours, great. But don't waste the rest of your time trying to look busy. Instead, be busy. Any manager worth his pay grade knows his workforce. So don't think that your fake industry is fooling him, or for that matter, anyone else. And really, why waste energy working at nothing when you can apply yourself and make a great impression? Go to your manager and say, "I've finished everything I was working on. What can I do to help?" You can even suggest where your talents might best be utilized—marketing, sales, public relations.

That extra effort almost certainly will mean more hours at the office. But when business is off, extra time behind your desk isn't such a bad thing. Being seen working after regular business hours is just politically smart when the market is bad. But let's say you are that super efficient and effective worker who flat out does more work in six hours than your colleagues can do in ten hours. If everyone else in your organization is logging extra hours and you're not, the boss is going to notice your absence, and not in a, "Boy, I'm sure glad Mike went home because he works so hard," kind of way. If your coworkers stay and you don't, not only do they win the perception-is-reality competition, but you have probably lurched ahead in the unemployment derby.

If you rise before the sun comes up and go into the office extra early, chances are your manager won't be there to greet you or see that you are logging those additional morning hours. Don't be shy. Make sure the people in power know that you are an early bird. Send your boss an e-mail. Leave a voice message. Drop off a note. It doesn't have to be elaborate. Just say, "I'm usually here around 7 each morning. If you need something done, just put it on my desk."

BE SUBTLE

Jeff Kaye, chief executive officer of Kaye/Bassman International, a Plano, Texas, recruiting firm, says it's not unusual for employees who work late to poke their heads into his office to say goodnight. In fact, he applauds their effort because he believes that it's important to master the art of getting noticed.

"The whole purpose wasn't to say goodnight," he says. "They wanted me to know that they were here until 7:30 P.M. It worked. I don't begrudge it. I respect it. Letting yourself be seen so that people who might not otherwise have any idea what you're doing know what you are doing—there's nothing wrong with that if you do it subtly."

2. Build a Reputation as a Hard Worker

Strive to make your brand synonymous with "hard worker." Developing that reputation starts with showing your manager and colleagues every day your pride and dedication to your job, the high quality of your work, and how, combined, they represent who you are as a person. In business, the people who are successful recognize that they are a brand and understand that they must protect and market that brand's reputation. To accomplish that you must:

✔ Consistently deliver what you promise.
✔ Be fair and ethical.
✔ Have personal integrity.
✔ Show people they can rely on you.

Once your brand is established, you want to remain in sync with your manager's or the company's goals. To do that, you must clearly understand what your manager expects from you, and, in turn, what kind of help you can expect from your manager. You can exchange that information through a framework of ground rules, or what can be called accountabilities and expectations. Having accountabilities and expectations in place makes it easier to track whether or not you are fulfilling your job responsibilities. Another way of thinking about accountabilities and expectations is as your personal mission statement. Every company has a written mission statement, a vision, and a set of core values that explains what it embodies. Most also list the company's goals and where it wants to go in the future. How many employees do you think have even taken the time to consider a personal mission statement, let alone define their values, career vision, and long-term professional goals? Very few. In fact, odds are better than even that you have never written down a personal mission statement. Well, now is the time to do it.

Building a framework of accountabilities and expectations begins with a detailed description of job responsibilities. Together with your manager, create a very specific, quantifiable list of precisely what each side can expect from the other. For instance, you, as the employee, might say you can be counted on to:

✔ Be at work every morning by 7 A.M.
✔ Return phone calls as promptly as possible, say within twenty-four hours.
✔ Be available in an emergency.
✔ Make a deadline once you have committed to a project and a timeline, and if you cannot meet the deadline let the supervisor know 72 hours in advance.

In turn, your supervisor might agree to:

✔ Tell you if you are not performing to a level exceeding expectations.
✔ Explain the gap between what you could be doing and what you are doing.
✔ Give you the opportunity to correct any deficiencies before letting you go.

When you have a list of agreed-upon points, each party should sign it. You can use the same process with the people who work with you and those who work for you. View your accountabilities and expectations as a way of measuring whether or not you are attaining the goals that you have set for yourself, and if you are receiving the right kind of feedback to correct any problems.

If your supervisor won't agree to a formal list of accountabilities and expectations, ask her to acknowledge these basic ground rules:

✔ If you don't hear anything from your manager, it means your work is fine.
✔ You cannot be demoted, fired, or otherwise punished for work if you have not been previously told what you are doing wrong.
✔ You will be given a chance to correct problems.
✔ Your manager must be accessible and willing to talk about issues.

BEING A HARD WORKER LEADS TO THE WHITE HOUSE

Before becoming a business consultant, Mary Crane attended the prestigious Culinary Institute of America. During a six-month externship at the world-famous Greenbrier resort in West Virginia, the executive chef told the students that they could use their time off to practice making different dishes at the Greenbrier's expense. Crane pounced on the opportunity, spending most of her free time in the kitchen. A few months after graduation, Crane got a call from the chef, who had moved to a new address—1600 Pennsylvania Avenue, in Washington, D.C. He asked Crane to join his staff because she had proven her dedication to cooking by giving up her private time to improve her skills while at the Greenbrier. He knew that she would deliver for him as a member of his White House cooking staff.

Crane spent two years as assistant chef at the White House, where she learned a lot about food, life, and literally putting out fires in the workplace. During a dinner on the White House lawn, Crane accidentally set a tablecloth on fire. The flames were quickly doused and Crane learned a little bit about how to deal gracefully with an unexpected workplace crisis.

3. Know When to Say No

When business is spiraling downward, you may be reluctant to decline a request from your manager to take on extra work. After all, you're one of the lucky ones who still has a job. Shouldn't you show your gratitude by taking on a pallet of extra work? It's completely understandable to think that way, but not necessarily smart. Sure, you should be flexible and open to helping out in any way you can. But you are, after all, human and have your limits. Moreover, employees who take on too much extra work actually put their jobs at more risk. Hauling the heavy load can cause a decline in the quality of your work. Deadlines may be missed, or problems covered up. What should you do? Be honest with yourself and your manager about what you can handle. After all, you won't help anyone if you overload yourself. And yes, it is tough to say no because you realize that the company is in trouble and that you were among the very few to be kept on. But if you don't set realistic boundaries, you won't be helping anyone. When your manager comes to you with yet even more work, don't be afraid to say, "Sorry, I've got all I can handle now and still do a good job. I just can't do another thing right now."

Your brand can help in this situation if it is universally acknowledged to represent hard work, high-quality standards, dedication, sincerity, and honor. People will accept that you are doing your best and not question your commitment. Your brand can also act like a compass, helping you decide which tasks you should take on, where to spend your time and energy, and with whom you should spend it.

One thing you don't want to do is assume extra work that hasn't been assigned by a manager because it may not be strategically relevant or immediately important. You may actually be unwittingly stepping on a political land mine. Perhaps even more importantly, you could be upstaging your manager.

If you can accept more work, figure out the best use of your talents and skills. Then go to your manager and volunteer your help. If your manager asks, tell her how you think you can best be utilized.

There is one last pitfall about knowing when to say no. If you continually agree to take on more and more work, somewhere along the line someone is going to start wondering about your job and why you always seem to have the time to take on extra work. And when a company is looking to cut costs, you can bet the house that your role and responsibilities within the organization will come under scrutiny. Your desk may be an avalanche of paper and work. You may be spending so much time at work that you are having your mail delivered to the office. But the people farther up the managerial chain looking for budget cuts to enhance the bottom line won't necessarily know that they are axing a work-horse from the organizational chart. By not combining the four-teenth and fifteen letters of the alphabet and uttering the word it creates, you may have inadvertently put your job at risk.

The moral of the tip: Just say no—occasionally.

4. Be a Low-Maintenance Employee

Every office has one: the prima donna who is always singu-larly accountable for his or her success, yet never responsible for any setbacks or failures. Nobody likes office jerks, but manage-ment will usually tolerate their ego-feeding antics because they are money makers or high performers. But the moment the mar-ket tanks or their numbers drop, the shield of profitability that has protected them from being fired dissolves. The bottom line is, if you insist on being a jerk you had better be one heck of a rain maker, particularly in bad times.

In an economic downturn you don't want the reputation of being a whiner—about anything from how much you make to the lack of hand towels in the bathroom. Drawing negative attention to yourself is beyond foolish. Instead, you want your manager to think of you as a rock of responsibility, someone that she can turn to in a crisis. So don't complain, pass blame, or spread rumors of rack and ruin when things are going badly. Instead, focus on the positive. Dig in and work harder as an individual and as part of a team. When times are difficult, your manager needs employees who can reduce her stress. You want to be that employee. Regardless of what everyone else in the office is doing, you deliver for your manager. You want to take on as much extra work as feasible. You want to make fewer errors than anyone else. And you want to make that extra client phone call or two or three, to show the manager that she doesn't have to spoon-feed you instructions on what to do next.

If you really want to make your manager smile while simultaneously lowering your maintenance quotient and keeping your job, just do the simple things. For instance, when your manager requests information, respond immediately. Managers hate having to repeatedly ask for budget numbers, progress updates, and other routine information. So, when you receive a behest from the boss, get working on it. If the inquiry comes via e-mail or voice mail, don't keep the manager wondering if you received the message. Pick up the phone, shoot back an e-mail, or stick your head into her office and say, "Hey, I got your request and I'm working on it." That small gesture means your manager doesn't have to worry about whether or not you are working on the issue or if you have any questions. But perhaps more importantly, by acknowledging the message, your manager considers you a responsible employee, someone they can depend on to do their job in a crunch.

Another way to buff your low maintenance bona fides and keep your job while everyone else around you is losing theirs, is to take a page from the Boy Scouts—Always Be Prepared. Finish your report or progress update with ample time to review it. Anticipate questions your manager may ask. Make sure that you have all the information necessary for a productive discussion. Nothing frustrates a manager more than conducting a meeting with people who have not done their homework. It makes you look bad. But more to the point, you look like you don't care.

Being a low-maintenance employee means being positive, dependable, responsible, and a team player, all of which make your manager's job easier in good or bad times. But in a shrinking economy, being a low-maintenance, highly productive employee vastly increases your chances of keeping your job.

5. Set High Standards for Yourself, and Then Exceed Them

With your accountabilities and expectations in place, set up a spread sheet listing your projects and personal goals. Track them by the week, month, and quarter. Doing so allows you to assess the current status of each project, where you can work to exceed management's expectations, and how the work can quantify your value to the company.

Say you have a project due next month. Make your goal to complete it two weeks early.

By bringing in the project early, your immediate manager will notice that you are working at a higher level and standard than your peers. Equally important, however, is that your stated and achieved goals and objectives, along with your standards of hard work and high quality, will translate into your value added to the company. And the people in power will notice.

Of course, with your commitment to setting and exceeding high standards expect some grousing among your peers. A friend once complained to Lisa Quast, president of Career Woman, about a new employee who she said was brown-nosing the manager. The friend said the new employee had met with everyone in the department, asking what they were working on. He used that information to develop a list of his own projects, which he gave to the manager. If that wasn't bad enough, the new employee started scheduling department meetings to update everyone on the progress of his projects.

When it came time for performance reviews, the new employee didn't wait for the manager, who was notorious for never conducting reviews, to schedule one. Instead the new employee wrote his own review, went over it with the manager, and had the manager sign it. He then photocopied the performance appraisal, had human resources put the original in his file, and kept the copy.

The friend was outraged by what her colleague had done. It was pointed out to this person that the new guy wasn't being a brown-noser. He was merely establishing his brand—as a hard worker willing to go above and beyond his job description for the betterment of the department and company—with his manager. If you were the manager, the friend was asked, and it came to a decision where you had to downsize one person, who do you think you would choose? Would it be someone who had been with the company for a while and was more or less on cruise control, or the new person who has been there six months and has a list of all his projects, goals, and objectives, where he was with each of those, and a performance appraisal on file?

The friend got the point.

STANDARDS CHANGE

Like just about everything else, the definition of high standards is constantly changing. What passed as setting the bar high ten or fifteen years ago may now be nothing more than an easy hop. Jeanine Tanner O'Donnell had a client who got caught in the time warp. The manager made it clear to her client that business was slow and employees needed to pick up their game and do it quickly. Rather than ask what he could do, O'Donnell's client simply ignored the warning, reasoning that he had risen to his current level because he so often had exceeded everyone's expectations.

O'Donnell urged him to do something strategic to show that he took the warning seriously. But just as he had turned a deaf ear to his boss, he disregarded O'Donnell's advice. The client was fired.

"You cannot assume that the patterns you witnessed over the past ten or fifteen years are going to be the same," O'Donnell says. "Don't assume your position is safe."

6. If You Make a Mistake, Own Up to It Quickly

To err is human. The urge to cover it up is even more so. When you make a mistake at work, no matter how foolish or costly, it is imperative that you own up to it immediately. Businesses today are so interconnected that hiding a mistake on your project may have adverse effects on work being done elsewhere in the company. And creating problems for colleagues because you were afraid or unwilling to say you goofed is a great way to destroy your brand, as well as make yourself a target for firing. So if you make a mistake, don't hem and haw, try to mitigate, or in any way shun responsibility, especially if you are the team leader. Standup people don't do that. What they do is have the courage to tell their manager about the mistake and then fix it by doing the following:

✔ Explain why you think the mistake was made.
✔ Assess the immediate damage done.
✔ Assess possible long-term damage.
✔ Lay out a plan to fix the problem.
✔ Turn the mistake into a learning opportunity.
✔ Put measures into place to make sure it doesn't happen again.

Will the price of owning up to the mistake be your job? Probably not. Will your boss be annoyed with you for a couple of days, perhaps a week, certainly no longer than a month? You bet. But he will also know that you can be trusted to do the right thing, regardless of the consequences. And because you reported it immediately and accepted responsibility, your brand will actually be stronger.

People often think they can fix a mistake on their own and that no one will ever be the wiser. Well, forget that idea. It is almost impossible to keep an important business mistake secret. Jane, the team leader of an information technology system integration project, found that out the hard way. Early in the project Jane became aware that the manpower and time needed to conduct system testing had been woefully underestimated. Rather than tell her boss and ask for help, Jane kept the mistake hidden and tried to work through the problem on her own. It wasn't long before cost overruns reached $250,000 and Jane had no choice but to reveal the mess to her boss.

The blindsided executive suddenly found himself explaining cost overruns to an Executive Steering Committee that thought everything was running smoothly. Needless to say, the committee members were not happy. Jane's failure to alert her boss immediately embarrassed him in front of the committee and made him look incompetent. Thankfully, the boss was able to redeem himself by recouping the lost money from other parts of the project.

When the dust settled, Jane's boss sat her down. He told her that she should never worry about making a mistake because he viewed mistakes as normal and a learning tool. He then explained that by not coming to him at the first sign of trouble, she allowed the mistake to grow and affect other areas of the project. Had she been upfront, the boss said, Jane would have earned points with him. She would have been given credit and acknowledged for her awareness and ability to identify problems.

7. Dress for Success

If you want to be treated like a professional, dress like one. How well, or not so well, you dress influences how people perceive you, which, of course, makes it part of your brand. And for many people, your boss and clients included, perception is reality. Whether fair or not, some people will judge you on what you wear and how you present yourself. You don't have to look like you stepped off a fashion runway or the pages of *GQ* magazine, unless, of course, you have an affinity for wearing and paying for labels with fancy names. But you do have to look the part. So make sure that you are in line with your industry's uniform. How can you tell if you have the correct look? Just dress like other people in your position or at your level. Failing to meet expectations can translate into lost business, lost respect, or worse, a lost job. Why? Because the perception people have is of the way somebody in your position typically looks. So, if your manager has two people and she must let one go, then perception holds a lot more weight than it otherwise might.

MEASURE UP, BUT JUST A LITTLE

Early in her career, Lisa Quast, founder and president of CareerWoman in Seattle, Washington, asked someone she admired what advice they had for her. The answer—always look professional. You do that, she was told, by observing how the people two levels above you dress, and then emulating that style.

"In other words, don't go all the way to the top," Quast says. "Go just a couple of levels above you, and look for any difference in how those people dress or look professionally. What happened then is when I got a promotion people would say, 'You really were always a cut above the rest.' A lot of that is just perception."

8. Use Colors to Convey the Right Message

Now that your wardrobe meets your profession's standards, it's time to learn a little about using colors to your advantage. It may seem hard to believe, but the color of your clothing can tell people a lot about how you feel and, to a certain extent, what you are doing that day. Studies have found that colors can actually affect the way people feel about themselves. But the color you wear can also influence the way people react to you. That is why, for instance, you will see many Western male world leaders, and the CEOs of big corporations, decked out in dark suits, accented with either a red or blue tie. Dark colors, especially black, are a sign of power, elegance, and mystery, while a red tie represents passion, excitement, and danger. Blue, on the other hand, signifies trustworthiness, peace, and loyalty.

The colors you choose, then, can save your job by giving you a psychological edge on the people you work with. Say there is a staff meeting that you know has the potential to be testy. You can select your wardrobe colors based on the reaction you want to elicit. For instance, if you want to be center stage, red is your color. Red is an attention grabber. It says, "Look at me. I am confident and self-assured." If you just want to cow your colleagues, you might select something dark—a black or dark gray. Maybe you want to be a calming presence at the meeting. In that case, add some green or earth tones to your ensemble.

Using colors is a little easier for women—when was the last time you saw a guy wearing a red blazer at work and wondered if he got dressed in the dark? But there are still some hard and fast rules. Business people who want to be taken seriously, men and women alike, dress in colors appropriate for the situation. For instance, a woman giving a presentation to the board of directors isn't going to show up in a hot pink suit or a screaming yellow outfit and not expect people to be distracted. No, she will most likely be wearing a dark gray, black, or dark blue conservative suit.

One last thing about appearance. Both men and women should also be careful about how they accessorize their outfits. For instance, if you are a woman entering an evaluation meeting with your manager, do you really want to be weighed down with gold or blinding him with the glint from the precious stones in your rings? If you are a guy, the last thing you want is your manager commenting on your ultraexpensive wristwatch. By paying attention and putting a little effort into the color selection of your outfits, you wardrobe can contribute to helping you save your job.

9. Blow Your Own Horn, But Never Too Loudly

Sometimes it pays to advertise, especially when your brand is the product and your manager is the customer. The trick, of course, is to do it subtly. If you receive a letter praising your work, make a few copies and give one to your manager and place another in your personnel file. If the letter is exceptional and comes from a prominent client, you might consider hanging it inside your cubicle or office. Again, you want to display the letter discreetly so that it draws peoples' attention without you mentioning it. For instance, you might want to situate the letter so that it will catch the eye of someone sitting in front of your desk. Don't go overboard. One or two neatly framed letters will suffice.

There are several pluses to blowing a mellow note or two from your horn. For one, it shows your manager that important customers admire your work and respect you as a business partner and person. And when done judiciously, it doesn't come off as arrogant or obnoxious. Finally, because you have skillfully reinforced your brand as an overall great employee and swell guy, you can be more generous in sharing credit with colleagues for jobs well done. Of course, that further burnishes your already gleaming brand while adding another layer of job security.

For whatever reason, trumpeting personal accomplishments seems to be something women are uncomfortable doing. In general, women have been socialized not to call attention to their successes. Bragging is, well, not ladylike. Women are consensus builders. They are "we" people, not "I." Good work matters. But what matters even more is that your boss knows about it. It is easier to let someone go if you are unfamiliar with their individual accomplishments. If you are always the quiet, unassuming person in the meeting, you can expect that when it comes time for layoffs your name is going to get mentioned.

As more women climb the rungs of the success ladder and settle into upper management postions, they are becoming acutely aware of the need to indulge in a little self-promoting. They understand it's their responsibility to tell the boss exactly what they are bringing, day in and day out, to the table. Instead of always promoting the team, more women are learning to refocus the spotlight on themselves. In today's business world, women know that they have to quantify and be precise about their contributions to projects. Women have to become comfortable saying, "I helped the project succeed by doing this."

Men are less likely to be inhibited and more artful when it comes to self-promotion. Take the case of Bill, a human resources manager for a large company who was part of an advisory committee charged with negotiating a new health care benefits contract.

Bill was the only committee member with experience negotiating health care contracts. So while committee members droned on meeting after meeting about how much they would pay for the benefit package, Bill was quietly meeting with the provider. A few weeks later he brought the board a contract proposal that included a seven percent reduction in premiums and administrative costs.

The committee was thrilled. When Bill wrote his report, he credited the hard work and negotiating skills of the committee for saving the company money. Bill then was asked to make a formal presentation to the company's top executives. Again, he lavishly praised the committee's hard work. He talked about how well "we" worked together, and the long hours "we" put in. It was a "we" fest. Only once did he mentioned how "I" convinced the provider to discount our premiums because of our long relationship.

The committee members, many of whom were senior level managers, knew that Bill could have played the entire performance in front of the executives as a solo. Instead he chose to play almost all harmony.

10. Add Technology to Your Brand

Technology is constantly changing and evolving. For business, that has meant a blink-of-an-eye transition from local, regional, and national markets, to global competition. But it is also an opportunity for employees with technology skills to add to their brand while increasing their job security.

When you share information online, whether it is writing a blog, hosting an industry website, or doing research that can be shared with colleagues, you attract people. For instance, if you write a blog that shares your experiences within the company or department, or takes on larger corporate issues, people will respond to you. The more respect your online work garners, the more valuable you become to the organization.

Ross Mayfield, President of Socialtext, knows firsthand how Internet skills can insure your job. Several years ago, he worked for a company advising the president of Estonia, a small Eastern European country. Mayfield was using the Internet to keep in touch with people at home. As his Internet expertise grew, he created a website for the Estonian president and taught him how to surf the web. The president was quite old, but he had a great intellect and tremendous curiosity about the Internet and kept Mayfield around to teach him.

Mayfield opened a LexisNexis account from which he took news clippings based on foreign relations topics and developed a foreign policy e-mail newsletter, which he redistributed inside the company.

The things Mayfield did for the Estonian president you can do today for almost no cost, with less work, and reach a much wider audience. But to do it, you must dedicate time to learning how to use today's technology so that when the opportunity arises, you will be able to take the initiative.

WEAVE A WEB OF TECHNICAL SKILLS

Perhaps no group understands the power and influence that comes with sharing knowledge and skills as well as technology-savvy employees. They freely share information in a variety of online forms, from blogs to websites. So make computer skills part of your brand.

"We are moving from a 'need to know' culture, to a 'need to share' culture," Mayfield says. "The more that you share, the more that your information can be leveraged by other people to create other things. When you share information, that information can be an attractor to you. So, a person that has a blog that is sharing their experiences in management, in their department, or larger corporate issues, is going to attract attention and become some level of celebrity within the organization."

People leverage their technology skills by doing web research, creating business-related online newsletters, writing company blogs, or managing an industry-oriented chat site. Many front office departments are shifting their work to the web. That means front office people need to know how to work on the web and know how to do everything from manage a site to reasonably respond to questions and comments. As a computer tech client of workplace consultant Jeanine Tanner O'Donnell once told her, he would never be fired because his boss had so many computer passwords that he couldn't keep them straight.

"I'll never lose my job," he told O'Donnell, "because I have all the knowledge."

11. Know When and How to Recast Your Brand

You already understand why simply being the hardest worker alone won't save your job in a significant downturn. You have to be the hardest worker at something that really matters to the company if you want to keep your job. So dodging the unemployment bullet may require recasting your brand.

If you work in a section of the company that is in flux, or the sales numbers are bad, or revenue is missing its projections, you have to do something positive that will make your manager notice you. And no, trying to fly under the radar until the worst has passed isn't a viable strategy. You have two choices—figure out what is going on in the organization and try to find someplace safer, or sit back and wait for the ax to fall. And it will fall. It's just a matter of when.

A business facing a downturn is like an airplane trying to gain altitude. Both target the dead weight, open the door, and toss it out. If your brand doesn't work in the company's future direction, well, get ready to be tossed out the door. Or, here's a thought: You can change your brand. Will people accept you doing that? You bet your job they will, if you do it right. Start your metamorphosis by learning everything you can about why the company is going in a new direction and where it expects to land. Get your hands on information like:

✔ Market data.
✔ Industry data.
✔ The competition's direction.
✔ Growth and development areas in your industry.
✔ Why your job doesn't fit in.
✔ What position is replacing what you do.

Talk to peers inside your company to get their take on what is going on, and sources outside to get an industry-wide view. Read industry magazines, newsletters, and websites to find out what is being done new and differently. What are the cutting-edge trends? Then, adjust your brand to match those differences. Now, identify which decision makers need to know about your new brand. Explain how the new-and-improved you dovetails with the company's new direction:

✔ Meet with people that you didn't meet with before.
✔ Write a report explaining how your job dovetails with the new direction.
✔ Hold a seminar or give a presentation outlining your job and the new direction.

To reposition your job, you must thoroughly understand what you want to do so that you can explain and quantify how it differs from what you are currently doing. Quantifying the difference will allow you to parallel the two jobs side-by-side. That way, in an easy-to-understand format, you can illustrate in dollars and cents what your current job contributes to the company's bottom line, and how, by repositioning your work, the contributions will be greater.

REBRANDING A DEPARTMENT

A department head whom Philip Berry, managing principal of Berry Block and Bernstein LLC, a New York consulting firm, knows was on the verge of losing his job because his group's product was losing market share. After carefully considering his alternatives, the man decided the answer was to change the department's brand. Rather than spend more money, his strategy was to cut advertising and production costs and contribute to the company's bottom line in that manner.

"His group was only focused on spend, spend, spend, and giving more to advertising," Berry says. "They turned the brand around. Instead of focusing just on advertising, they were able to do it on a cost savings factor without cheapening the product."

The plan worked, and over time the department head earned a reputation—brand—for being able to squeeze extra nickels and dimes out of his budget without reducing the quality of the product.

12. Check Your Personal Life, Not Your Personality, at the Door

When business is going bad, you need to focus all your energy and attention on keeping your job. Anything short of life and death—literally—goes on the back burner while you navigate the Straits of Unemployment. Tell your husband, wife, children, significant other, even the dog, that, right now, you must put extra effort in at work. When business is bad and jobs are on the line, nonpressing personal issues have to come second. It is critically important during a down cycle that you are seen at the office. The more face time you have with your manager, the better his or her impression.

While personal issues should take a back seat, don't check your personality at the door. Your personality is the vivaciousness of your brand. It is what shows how much you enjoy your job. It is why you are nice to your colleagues. It contributes to your being a low-maintenance team player. And you do, after all, spend a large chunk of your week with the people at work. Why wouldn't you want to get to know them and invite them to know the real you? True, many experts believe you are better off separating your personal life from who you are at work. But others don't see the benefit of that approach. Many business people believe that fraternizing or becoming friends with coworkers forms an important bond. Plus acting one way at work and another in your private life almost requires you to have a dual personality.

Showing people the real you has lots of benefits, unless of course you actually are a prima donna or don't understand the difference between confidence and arrogance. Letting your colleagues see the person you are away from work takes you from being a one-dimensional employee to a human being, with a whole array of interests, some of which you might share. And, believe it or not, sharing that information may just save your job when everyone else is losing theirs.

"When I have a deeper personal relationship with those I work with, doesn't it make it harder to fire them?" Kaye asks. "Now I am not just firing Jeff. I am laying off Jeff, which I know is going to have an impact on Sally and their two kids. My recommendation would be that in order to build an effective career, one would need to insure and understand that there is nothing wrong with allowing your personal life and your professional life to blend into one another, as long as when you are at your job you engage in professional activities."

MATCHING YOUR JOB TO YOUR PERSONALITY

How your personal life melds with how you handle work demands is something you should resolve long before you find yourself fighting to keep your job. Every organization has a mission statement, a set of values that comprises its world view or culture. Ideally, your personal values should mesh with that world view. You should feel proud of the company you work for and enjoy being there. If you don't, you will find working for the company difficult, and even unpleasant, and you either will quit, or be fired. So, before saying "yes" to a job offer, do your homework. Read about the company and its founders. Understand the company's mission and how it intends to fulfill its goals. Then sit back and ask yourself if your values are consistent with the organization's culture and values. For instance, if you are a family-first person, does the company share that value? If the answer is no, then think long and hard because the job may not be the right fit for you.

13. Think Like a Chess Player

If you want to build a successful career, think like a chess player. World-class chess players aren't thinking about their next move—they're thinking several moves ahead. And that, say experts, is the way you should think about building your career while keeping your job.

You always have to be aware of what is going on around you so that you aren't blindsided and suddenly lose your job. That is your short-term plan. Your long-term design should look five years ahead to where you want to go and what moves you have to execute to get there. Part of that plan is understanding how your current job contributes to your ultimate plan. Chess's grand masters don't reach that supreme level playing the game one move at a time. Neither should you. Start sketching out your strategy by asking:

✔ Where do you want to be in five years?
✔ Why do you want to be there?
✔ What are you willing to do to reach your goal?

Write down the answer to each question and use it like a navigational chart to make sure your heading stays true. Use your accountabilities and expectations for course corrections as you sail along. You will find that once your vision, mission, values, and course heading are in place, the trip to your destination will become much easier.

As you sharpen the focus of your career plan, always be mindful of the senior management people who are involved in your areas of interest. It is easy enough to do. Start by reading the company's annual report or visiting its website to make sure that your career goals are still aligned with your employer's stated goals. Now find out who are the people in charge a level or two above you. Take your investigation one more step and try to evaluate each person's overall importance and value to the company. Now try to figure out a way that you can get connected to the managers who appear to have deep company ties and long-term staying power.

Building your career is about hard work and having a long-term plan. It's also about building relationships, networking, and knowing who has power and who has lost power. Some people may accuse you of being self-serving or disloyal for managing your career with those calculating measurements. Of course you are self-serving. It is your career. As long as you aren't a jerk or underhanded in any way, there is nothing wrong with being aware of what is going on around you. The only other choice you have is to put your head down and hope for the best. How many chess grand masters do you think would endorse that strategy? Well, when it comes to your career, neither should you.

CHECK MATEY

The career moves you make today must align with your ultimate goal, otherwise you will never get where you want to go. That is why you must plan your future moves well in advance. Jeff Kaye likens careers to aircraft carriers. Both are big and neither can turn on a dime.

"You just don't decide to go left and the aircraft carrier goes left," says Kaye, CEO of Kaye/Bassman International, a Plano, Texas, recruiting firm. "You decide miles before that turn happens, or else it is not going to go where you want it."

14. Work at a Level or Two Above Your Position

Working a level or two above your position means investing time learning the issues that middle and senior managers face every day. So do your research. Read leadership and management books. Talk to the people above you. And then think, act, and ask questions like you are working a level or two above your job. You can meet people outside your realm by:

✔ Asking your boss for an introduction.
✔ Taking every opportunity to talk to people higher up.
✔ Sending an e-mail asking to meet.

In general, managers and executives are happy to talk to an employee who shows initiative and interest. When you meet with managers above your level, be respectful but not shy. Make the most of the opportunity. When you see someone on the elevator you would like to meet, politely introduce yourself. An important part of building your career is not being reluctant to ask for help.

Meeting and talking to the right people is just one aspect of working above your level. Once you understand the type of problems people above you face day-to-day, you must learn different strategies for working problems, consensus building, and how decisions are ultimately reached.

An upper-level manager realizes that most of his directives have far-reaching implications. So he must always take into account the entire company, and in some cases, industry environment, along with the interests of the stakeholders involved throughout the company and on beyond. Often, he must shelve the best idea in favor of a consensus plan to ensure that the company moves forward.

When you begin to understand how the world a level or two above you works, you will begin to appreciate the need to build corporate and political alliances. If you are smart, you begin constructing the bridges before you begin the work. Linda, a window/floor display designer for a well-known clothes designer, understands what it takes to work several levels above her job.

Linda was charged with creating a clothing display—called a "rig" in the industry—for a mall department store. She understood that her display would affect the way other people did their jobs. Wanting her display to be valuable for her company and the department store, Linda decided to find out what the people, the stakeholders, working in the store expected. So Linda met with the store's floor manager, the department store's buyers, and the clerks. She even called on the legal department to make sure the display met safety regulations.

Rather than say, "My job is to put up a display and that is all I am responsible for," Linda instead talked to everyone involved. After the meetings, she drew up a sample design and solicited input from everyone on ways to change or improve the design. When the display went up, the staff was happy and made sure that the display was well maintained. By taking the time to get input and buy-in from the staff, Linda was acting like a manager, which is several levels above her job.

MAKE THE MOST OF YOUR TIME

One way to work above your level is to use your time efficiently. For instance, when you are delayed at the airport, the computer server crashes, or it's a slow day at the trade show, don't sit around chatting with your colleagues. If you want to move ahead, view down time as an opportunity to get a head start on another project. And remember, down time at work is still company time.

15. Build Skills for Job Security

Continually upgrading and refining your skills is fundamental to keeping your job. The more business and industry knowledge you own, the more valuable and indispensable you become. So, accept every opportunity the company offers to expand your training. But don't limit yourself to company-sponsored classes. It's your career. Pay for a course or seminar that will help you at work. Pick and choose the classes you need to stay ahead of the game by:

✔ Tracking economic trends.
✔ Charting the company's direction.
✔ Matching your training with the company's goals.
✔ Keeping abreast of new technology.

Those tips may have been enough to secure your position a decade or so ago. In fact, just doing some of those things would have made you the go-to person in the office. But not anymore. In today's job market, simply keeping your skills current won't stop the boss from feeling badly as he lets you go during hard economic times. The key to keeping your job is understanding how to leverage your skills and knowledge. You do that by making yourself someone the company can least afford to lose.

"You have to take courses and keep your skills current," says Fran Landolf, a Baltimore-based business consultant. "But then you have to have the ability to leverage that knowledge to create a solution, and that means influencing people to do the things that need to be done."

An employer faced with letting people go is more likely to keep the employee who uses his or her skills and knowledge to influence others and drive opinions. Managers are especially impressed with people who can do it without being in a position of power. Why? Along with showing leadership qualities, they understand how to communicate and motivate their colleagues to get the job done. The bottom line is they are the company's future. And which company do you know that willingly gets rid of its future leaders? Executives understand the importance of employees who can influence others without the benefit of a position of power. What distinguishes those people is that they have what it takes to help a company survive the bad times so it can thrive and move to the next level during good times.

The easiest way to gain influence is to possess the knowledge other people want or need. But since almost everyone has some level of advanced training, knowledge alone isn't enough. You must also have the respect and trust of your coworkers. Those ingredients distinguish the person who is critical to the company's future in times of trouble from the exceptional person who the manager is reluctant to let go because they represent the company's future.

So, how do you use your skills and knowledge to secure a place in the company's future? First, show everyone that you have the knowledge by traveling the traditional training route and taking outside classes. But also volunteer to write reports, work on white papers, author journal articles, give speeches, and make presentations. Always make sure your manager knows everything you're doing to improve yourself professionally. Then, in every way possible, brand yourself as an expert. Your manager will be watching to see if your coworkers:

✔ Seek you out for your knowledge or skill.
✔ Listen to what you say.
✔ Are motivated and react to what you say.
✔ React to the knowledge/skill or your personality.

Once you have established your skills and expertise, give it away freely to anyone who wants it. Let people know that you are a willing resource. Your manager will appreciate your willingness to share and admire your self-confidence and leadership qualities.

16. Become the Expert in Your Field

If you really want to stand apart from your colleagues while protecting your job, become your organization's resident expert. The mantle of expert is bestowed the old-fashioned way—you earn it. You do that by soaking up, digesting, and employing every iota of information about your field. So read, watch, write about, and listen to everything you can get your hands, eyes, and ears on concerning your industry or the specialized aspect of your job. Attend lectures, conventions, and symposiums, even if you have to pay your own way. Join industry-related organizations and clubs. Blog online about your business interests. Give presentations and speeches. Author articles and develop PowerPoint presentations.

"Any time you can become an expert in an area, you become the person that everyone goes to for information, and that immediately makes you invaluable," Mary Crane, president of Mary Crane & Associates, says. "So join organizations or make sure they are aware of your existence and that you are an expert in a particular field."

Most people don't consciously strive to become experts. They attain that level of respect because their interest in the field transcends their job. Their work becomes a way of life that they continue to develop and explore. With today's tight marketplace, it would behoove you to ask yourself how you can become the go-to person in your field for your company. You could probably learn something from Nancy, a basic business trainer who became her company's employee assessment expert.

Nancy's job was developing and teaching training programs for her company. But what she really enjoyed was doing leadership and management assessments. One day she walked into her manager's office and announced that her professional goal was to be the company's assessment expert. She said that she wasn't seeking a raise, didn't want a promotion, would gladly continue performing her current job, and didn't expect the company to pay for her advanced education. All she wanted was the chance to do management assessments after she was properly certified. Her manager thought the idea was great. He said if she took the classes and got certified she could pursue her dream.

Over the ensuing months Nancy spent her own money to get certified in the three leading assessment instruments. She created a series of pilot courses to see if there was an interest at work. There was. To prove the classes were beneficial, Nancy analyzed her findings and presented the results in a report.

Meanwhile, she also joined national and local assessment organizations to start building a professional network. And Nancy took more courses.

At work she was a one-person marketing group. She produced and sent out to every department a series of one-page white papers that outlined the value of assessments and offered some how-to tips. Then she visited every group in the company and asked to speak at each department's meeting. All the while she continued to do her job developing and teaching basic training courses.

It paid off. Today Nancy is the company's assessment expert. She has her own group of employees who do nothing but assessment programs.

17. Learn the Language

Every industry has its own vernacular. Information technology is littered with acronyms. Medicine is laced with Latin and Greek. Law is, well, law. Your job is to learn the language of your industry that has been developed over generations. You can learn it by going to business school. Most of the people in business schools innately know the principles they are studying. What they don't understand or know how to use is the vocabulary of business terms and phrases—*operational efficiency, bottom-line revenue, shareholder value,* and *price-to-earnings ratio* are usually not part of most individuals' everyday conversations.

Unless you are going to business school for the credential, there is another, less expensive way to learn the language of your commerce: Simply pay attention and then imitate the language. Listen to the vocabulary and word combinations your bosses use when they talk to each other about business issues. You want to use the same words in the same manner and context as the people you report to, and the people they report to. During a presentation, take note of the particular way the CEO describes an issue. Absorb the cadence of the words and phrase in the sentence. Great speakers deliver sentences with a rhythm. Your boss or CEO may not be a great speaker, but they usually have a good command of industry and business vocabulary. Listen and then practice using the terminology.

The payoff is that when you use a business term or phrase correctly in conversation, you not only sound like the boss, but you sound like someone who understands the business. And if the boss just happens to be in earshot of your conversation, she recognizes the language and may even be complimented if she hears a term she has used or introduced.

Parroting the bosses can help you stay employed in a down economy, because it is just one more way of differentiating yourself from your peers. You are showing the power brokers that you recognize the broader context of how the business operates and understand the value of what you do in the organization. It leaves the very clear impression with them that you understand the complex relationships that exist in the workplace environment. Simply put, you are talking about business in terms that make sense to senior managers.

Do you know what a *spaver* is? Well, neither did the people attending a recent business seminar. From the looks on the attendees' faces, the speaker realized that no one had ever heard of the term. So he explained: A *spaver* is actually the fusion of "spending to save." So a *spaver* is someone who spends money now in order to save money over the long run. For instance, a *spaver* pays a large chunk of money to completely upgrade a plumbing system today rather than pay smaller sums to a plumber to fix leaks as they occur over a longer period of time.

One last thing concerning language: For it to be effective, you must speak at the level of the person you are addressing. How you talk to the boss or the boss's boss is not the way you speak to the loading dock supervisor. One understands the concept of price-to-earnings ratio while the other is more invested in shipping capacity and worker hours. Think of it as a different dialect of the same language.

18. Learn a Second Language

Learning a second language is just about the sturdiest career-building, job-saving advantage you can have in today's world economy. Every global company covets employees who are fluent in a foreign language, whether it is Spanish, Chinese, German, Persian, or Arabic. Even smaller companies, if given the choice, will add an employee with another language.

An employee with language skills brings a lot to the table. For one, being fluent in a language usually requires being immersed in the culture. So now, as an employer, you have someone who not only can converse in the language, but understand important cultural differences, like say the difference in how business is done in Mexico compared to Colombia. Or she can explain to you the way you should present your business card to your Japanese counterpart.

An employee fluent in a foreign language also understands the nuances of language usage. That can come in handy and help avoid those embarrassing moments, like when a company uses a word from a foreign language to name their product because the executives think it means something innocent, when locally the word is used to describe an embarrassing part of a man or woman's anatomy. That has happened more than once.

Being fluent in another language will allow you to take on more responsibilities during business trips. You can act as the company's ad hoc translator during business meetings or at a restaurant. You can write letters and e-mails, or proofread outgoing communications for cultural, as well as spelling mistakes.

So, if your company offers any language courses, or programs about respecting, promoting, and learning about cultural differences, get involved. By being proactive you will show your boss that you want to grow and become more involved in the business and its global future.

DON'T LEAVE HOME WITHOUT ONE

As a health care consultant working on a global project, Lisa Quast spends a lot of time overseas. She knows firsthand the real value of having an employee who speaks foreign languages. In fact, she has one employee who is fluent in three languages and is almost fluent in two others.

"He's incredibly valuable," says Quast, founder of Career Woman, Inc. "If we had to downsize and it was between him and someone else who does not speak other languages but otherwise has the same skills, I would absolutely go with the person with the multiple languages. In today's global economy, being able to speak another language is incredibly valuable."

19. Quantify Your Value

If the value of your work can be translated into cold, hard, positive numbers, you will keep your job when everyone around you is losing theirs. But don't expect your boss to do it for you. It is your responsibility to show your manager and his managers how much your job contributes to the company's bottom line in dollars and cents.

Every job has a set of goals and objectives, usually laid out by the department manager. For instance, if your job is to run training programs, your boss may expect you to design and conduct fifteen programs and graduate 300 people a year. Or say you are an accountant charged with processing invoices. Someone higher in the food chain probably has developed a set of metrics to determine how many invoices you should handle per day, week, or month. A timeliness factor and error rate may also be built into the job's goals and objectives.

To keep your job, you can't just monitor and meet those goals and objectives. You must exceed them. You can do that by asking yourself how your job can benefit the company's bottom line. Think through ways you can convert your work into tangible, real-world results.

That's what Jim did when he took an internal corporate staffing job. Jim realized that it was not the most glamorous job in the business world. Still, he was determined to show his manager that he was bringing value to the company. To that end, Jim sat down and documented every person he was recruiting. Then he calculated what it would cost the company to hire an outside agency to contact and recruit the same number of people. When the ciphering was completed, he compared it to his salary and discovered that he was saving the company $1.5 million a year.

Pretty darn good work, but Jim went another step. He looked at the people he had successfully recruited into the business. It turned out that he was responsible for hiring twenty-seven of the top thirty-two people in his division. His work had completely changed the face of the organization. Jim wrote up everything and presented it to his manager. His manager was so bowled over by the numbers that he gave Joe a bonus and promotion.

By creating a way to establish his value to the company in such a graphic way, Jim was protecting his job while advancing his career. You should do the same. But many employees assume that managers already know the bottom-line value of each position. Consequently, they don't take the time to quantify their work. That's a huge, but common mistake. Managers may have the raw numbers, but they probably haven't had the time or inclination to dissect or digest the data, especially if the business is in trouble and scrambling.

So be like Jim and, prior to your performance review, write up an appraisal using your detailed records. Compare the job's agreed-upon goals and objectives with your documented performance. Maybe your job won't save the company millions, but keeping a detailed record of your work will help you stay focused so that you can exceed those preordained targets. More importantly, you will have a set of documented facts that you can present to your manager during a performance review.

REMIND YOUR MANAGER ABOUT THE LITTLE THINGS

Sometimes the little things that aren't directly tied to your job's goals and objectives count for a lot. So make sure you get credit for the kinds of contributions that can slip between the cracks. For instance, perhaps you developed a new, more efficient way to process invoices, which the company implemented and consequently saved money. Or maybe it had nothing at all to do with your job. Perhaps you found a place to hold the annual conference and save the company a bundle of money. Use the little things to illustrate that you are exceeding your job's goals and your manager's expectations. Again, don't expect your manager to remember anything. Document what you suggested and how it saved the company money. And then remind your manager about it during your performance review.

20. Volunteer for Assignments

Draw attention to yourself and your work by volunteering for assignments. Mind you, not just any assignment. Volunteer for challenging projects that will stretch your experience and have the potential to make you a star. Sure, it will be a little scary standing center stage in the hot glare of the spotlight as you work on something you've never done before. But just the fact that you were willing to enter the cage with an eight-hundred-pound gorilla will impress people enough to cut you some slack.

To increase your chances of success, read and learn everything you can about your given project. Then touch base with other people in the organization who have worked on similar projects. You will want to make them your allies. Also, find a senior manager—not your manager or anyone connected to the project—who will give you honest feedback and suggest course corrections when needed. Finally, make sure you and your manager are on the same page about the project. Get as many details about the results your manager expects. Ask what resources she will make available to you, and a pledge of accessibility and open communication. Getting a commitment means your manager is invested in the project and will make time for you.

Roy Roper knows a little about taking on a project that was way out of his depth. As a young man, Roper volunteered to oversee the conversion of a small East Coast operating facility into a regional service center, 3,000 miles from the company's headquarters in California. He had never done anything like it before, but was determined to meet the challenge. Plus, he knew that successfully completing the assignment would put a shine on his already rising star.

As luck would have it, things started out badly. A key person who was supposed to accompany Roper east immediately dropped out of the project. Roper knew he should ask for a replacement but decided instead to go it on his own. With no other managerial help, Roper was spread tissue-paper thin. He had to close one office and merge it with another to create a regional center. He solicited the support of the people in the two offices he was merging. He also met with customers to reassure them, and held sessions with the workers who would be most affected by the merger. In retrospect, Roper says he would have done some things differently. He made some bad hiring decisions that were counterbalanced by the good people he hired. And he got dinged on some operational issues that he wasn't familiar with. But he didn't lose one customer.

"I made some mistakes," he says. "I had good credibility inside the company and people trusted me. I leveraged the reputation I had in order to build a bigger one. I took the risk and pulled it off and, in the end, got a promotion out of it."

21. Attend Meetings

Meetings have long been the bane of organizational life. People are consumed with agreeing to meetings, scheduling meetings, and writing reports about meetings. Yet most of the time when they go to meetings, they're not fully attentive.

In a good economy, the importance of going to meetings depends on how vital they are to your job. Of course, if your manager asks you to make an appearance, you go, end of story. But if you work in a very political environment, you might want to weigh the benefits. For instance, if 95 percent of what you do is known and easily quantified, making a meeting isn't as pivotal.

But when business is in a downturn, meetings take on a whole new, absolutely significant tone. Meetings are your primary source of visibility to groups of people you may not normally encounter. The bottom line is that in today's job environment, meetings have taken on new relevance. Your manner and how you engage during the meeting will not only determine what you get from it, but also your value to the company. So grab a soft cushion and top off your coffee mug because you will be going to a lot of meetings. And you had better be awake, alert, and up to speed. In case you forgot, here are the rules of the road:

- ✔ Don't contradict your boss.
- ✔ Don't lose your temper.
- ✔ Don't attack anyone, either verbally or physically.
- ✔ Don't attack other people's ideas.
- ✔ Go with an open mind.
- ✔ Listen carefully so you can pick up the direction.
- ✔ Add something constructive.
- ✔ Don't talk for the sake of talking.
- ✔ If you can't add something constructive to say, keep mum.
- ✔ Think before you speak.

If you're new to a company and its meeting style, keep quiet and observe until you know the players and get the lay of the land. When you're ready to participate, do some prep work. Find out who called the meeting and why, and what results they hope to achieve. The more about the meeting you know, the better the contribution you can make, so:

✔ Find out who else will be in the meeting.
✔ Talk to your boss about it.
✔ Know the hot political issues so you don't trip over one.
✔ Understand the needs and wants of the other participants.

Attending a meeting is just the first step. You are there because someone thinks that you can add an idea and strategy that will help move the topic forward. Don't disappoint them. A meeting is a fantastic opportunity to promote your brand and build your career. You want the other participants to see you as someone who is interested, prepared, curious, and a knowledgeable problem solver.

By being prepared and giving a good accounting of yourself at a meeting, you significantly lighten the load on your boss, while earning points. Now take the next step. Volunteer to do some postmeeting follow up. It will show that you are a valuable, involved member of the team who is willing to go the extra mile for the company.

GOING THE EXTRA SEVERAL HUNDRED MILES

Jack's company recently moved its quarterly meeting from New York to Chicago. The agenda looked pretty mundane and nothing of significance was expected to happen, so Jack was told that he didn't have to fly out. Jack double-checked the agenda and, sure enough, the topics were not out of the ordinary. The issue was settled and Jack called a colleague to say he wasn't coming out. The colleague was surprised and told Jack that there was no way given the current business environment that he would miss an opportunity to be seen, no matter how pedestrian the agenda. Why pass up a chance to be in the same room with the CEO and other senior managers? The next morning Jack booked his flight to Chicago.

22. Prepare for Meetings

Now that you recognize the importance of attending meetings, how do you prepare to get the most from one? Let's say you are readying for a department budget meeting. In that case, you need to:

✔ Know the specifics about your part of the budget.
✔ Know the overall department budget.
✔ Know the budget comparison between the last period and now.
✔ Think through any problems you see.
✔ Be prepared to discuss items that stand out.

Prepare for a meeting by gathering all the pertinent information concerning your area of the budget. Make sure that your facts and figures are spot-on accurate. Revisit the minutes of the last meeting to refresh your memory and to see where your budget then compares to where it is now. Investigate any discrepancies. If you flagged the problem, so will your boss. Gather the people who report to you and search for the answer. Then, in the meeting, call attention to the difference before your manager does. That will show her that you did your homework. But also have a detailed answer prepared that explains the difference.

Next, look at the overall department budget so that you understand how your section fits into the bigger picture. If you see problematic areas, sit down and talk it over with your peers. Brainstorm ideas and strategies to address each issue that arises. You want to be able to follow the discussion no matter which direction it turns.

Create and deliver an agenda several days ahead of time. At the very least, send out a page with topic headlines. Attach any relevant reports, progress updates, or other information. Issuing an agenda serves several purposes, not the least of which is to give the meeting a formal structure. But it is also a subtle way of giving your manager a "heads up" in case he has forgotten or been too busy to bone up on the topics. He will appreciate the gesture.

If it is a standing weekly or monthly department meeting, you should know what to expect, making it easier for you to anticipate your manager's needs. Get necessary reports or information to him in advance. Also, after you submit your report, leave a short note—"I sent you my reports and I'm ready for the meeting"—with his assistant.

By responding quickly and following up, you are showing an awareness of what is going on beyond your little piece of the company's universe. It also tells your manager that you are a responsible, self-motivated, self-managing, and low-maintenance employee that can be depended on in a crisis.

Experienced managers who have conducted scores of meetings say that the smoothest run meetings are those with employees who were prepared, issued an agenda and the necessary background materials in advance, and offered ideas and solutions to problems.

One final thing about meetings: At the end of a meeting, never give your manager a to-do list. The last thing your manager needs to do is chase down follow-up information. Instead, you do the work. It may not seem like much, but it will stick with your manager that you possess the qualities the company wants when they are deciding whom to keep on.

23. Learn to Give a Good Presentation

If you want to keep your job, learn how to give peerless presentations. If you think that means being an expert on your topic, you're only half right. Certainly you want people to respect your authority on the subject. But giving outstanding presentations is equally about how well you deliver your message.

Most people organize their presentations in a linear fashion. The presenter goes step-by-step, PowerPoint-page-by-PowerPoint-page, painstakingly leading people through the text and graphs on the screen until, finally, she reaches the main point or message at the end. The logical progression, shower-them-with-data-and-analysis method is preferred by nine out of ten science and technology people. That said, you've probably sat through your share of those types of presentations, regardless of your business. Do you remember how long it took you to drift off—maybe three minutes? Or did they lose you at "Hello?" And if you didn't know why the presentation was being given, would you remember its main point?

The people who give the best presentations understand that you must:

✔ Give your main point up front.
✔ Know who is in the audience.
✔ Use a lively mix of text and graphics.

If you are looking for a great example of how to design your presentation, read a good newspaper story. Journalists know that readers are an impatient lot. So you have to grab them quickly with a strong, punchy, information-filled lead. The first sentence of a good hard news story includes the who, what, when, where, how, and why of the incident. If you stop there and don't read another word, you still have the story's vital information. Even feature writers, who usually don't use the five Ws and an H lead, tell their readers by the second paragraph (called a nut graph) the story's main point.

Try a similar strategy the next time you are preparing a presentation. Think of your audience as fidgety readers. Instead of one sentence, you have just a couple of minutes to pull them into your presentation. Wait too long to snag them, and they're sleeping with their eyes open. So make your presentation crackle in the first few minutes. Deliver your message with crisp headlines and graphics. And then, for good measure, follow up with a nut graph–type summary page.

As you move into your presentation, you want to keep your audience engaged. You must understand that people receive and process information in different ways. For example, some are visually oriented, while others learn best by reading. The Myers-Briggs Type Indicator, first published in 1962, is a widely used and accepted tool that defines how people see the world and make decisions. The MBTI measures people's responses along four continuums:

✔ Extroversion vs. introversion.
✔ Sensing vs. intuition.
✔ Thinking vs. feeling.
✔ Judgment vs. perception.

Keeping your audience involved in your presentation means including something that addresses each type of learner. Let's take a thumbnail glance at MBTI types, starting with extroverts, who, as you might have guessed, have no problem giving their opinion. Extroverts like a lively discussion. Introverts, on the other hand, quietly think about things. So you must draw out introverts by asking questions.

Sensing that people generally are fact-based, strait-laced analytical types, with intuitive people developing their own conclusions from their sense of the situation and circumstances, so your presentation has to contain quantifiable information, while still tapping into the imagination.

Thinkers make decisions based on facts and a logical rationale. People who are more feeling oriented make their decisions based on how it will affect other people. They want to make sure that whatever is done will create harmony. Judgment people need agreement, closure, and a clear path forward. Perception people couldn't care less about a plan. They want to explore new ideas, options, and possibilities. So your presentation should include what is possible and options to explore.

Don't try to consciously consider each of these personality types while developing your presentation. Simply be aware that they exist, and when you are asked to give a presentation, know that you will be talking to a diverse audience. So change it up and keep it lively. Your goal is to have people remember and understand your main point.

24. Create a Work Network

Building a strong network will help you keep your job in a bad market, not because you know people, but because people up and down the chain of command know you. The more people who are exposed to your brand and the high quality of your work, the better your chances of someone speaking up for you when the bosses discuss layoffs. Plus, with contacts littered throughout the company, you're bound to hear whispers about what is going on well before employees with less of a network.

Start constructing your professional network from the first day on the job. Take the time to go around and meet your coworkers. Find out about their jobs and the projects they are working on. Be interested and friendly. If the person isn't immediately connected to your group, ask if it is all right to touch base every so often. Then exchange e-mail addresses and telephone extensions. Even if you just meet one new person a day, your network construction is underway.

Who should be in your network? Everyone, really. But at the very least, anyone involved in your business or industry that you have met directly or know through someone else. A big part of building a good, diversified network is wrangling introductions to the people your friends and colleagues know. Remember Tip Number 41: Be Civil to Your Colleagues? Well, network building is a great reason to adhere to that philosophy. People will acquaint you with their friends, colleagues, or outside contacts only if they believe you are a good person.

Your network should include people from all levels of the company—senior managers, managers at the level above you, your manager, peers, and junior department members—and from different departments and parts of the organization. Don't overlook the receptionist and janitor. You would be surprised how much they know about what's really shaking the ceiling tiles inside the executive suites.

In the old days (in technology time, that is a few years ago), building a professional network required doing a lot of leg work. It meant searching out people at breakfast meetings, seminars, and conferences and then keeping in touch with them via the telephone, a snail-mail note, or a quick lunch. But with online sites like LinkedIn, Facebook, and MySpace, as well as industry-specific sites, networking is much less labor intensive. LinkedIn, for instance, claims 25 million professionals from 150 countries. You can build your network by asking people to connect to you.

When they do, you are then permitted to view all of their connections, and in turn, all of the people they know.

Like road repairs, a network is never finished. You should always be expanding. At the same time, learn to use your contacts. Tap into their experience and industry smarts, especially in a down market. Don't be afraid to ask people for advice. Also, use your office network as a Global Positioning System for inhouse opportunities.

Networks, like many of those roads continuously in need of repair, are two-way systems. So when someone in your network asks you for advice or help, be generous. And if you know of a job or tidbit of information that will benefit someone in your network (and doesn't violate any rules or business ethics), let him know.

"Nothing works better than being a good connector of others," says Jennifer Berman, of CBiz Capitol Services. "If you are good at being proactive and saying, 'I know of a great opportunity for you,' that will come back to you tenfold."

25. Create a Nonbusiness Network

Don't limit your network to colleagues at work or in the industry. Everyone you meet has the potential to be an important part of your network. The people you socialize with, play sports with, or worship with have a wide array of family, friends, and colleagues who may be able to help you somewhere down the line.

You should consider every social engagement as an opportunity to network. No one is suggesting that you walk into every party pumping hands and handing out your business card like a hyperactive politician, although you should always carry your business card. At any social event there is a wonderful mix of people and professions. After all, the single most frequently asked question has to be, "So, Justin, what do you do for a living?"

Some social events are designed for networking. Take golf outings, for instance. Now did you really think the initial purpose of golf was sport? Of course not. It is a little known fact that golf was created by a Scotsman who wanted to expand his network to increase his bagpipe sales. In any case, golf outings with colleagues in your industry are a great way to build your network. Some professional organizations arrange trips to ball games, the theater, or the orchestra.

Another invaluable social networking tool is right on your desk. It is your personal address book. Page through and look for people you have lost contact with. Give them a call or shoot off a quick e-mail. You might even send them a white paper you wrote or information on a new program you are working on. The person, first of all, will probably be happy to have the contact re-established. And she may find your white paper or project interesting enough to tell someone in her network.

Social network connections can happen in the most unexpected times and places. Jennifer Berman, managing director of CBiz Capitol Services, doesn't sit in any school carpool lane. But her friend does, and one day Berman's friend started talking to another parent who happened to work for a large company. The company was undergoing some changes and was searching for someone with Berman's skills. The man gave the mom Berman's contact information, and the two did business together.

"People don't think about the fact that when they are in the carpool lane every day picking up their kids, that is a network," Berman says.

26. Always Carry a Business Card

Carrying a paper business card in the age of technology may seem downright archaic. But those old-fashioned cards still play an important role when it comes to making business connections. And really, is there an easier way to get your name and phone number in front of people? In business and social situations, a business card is a handy, inexpensive networking tool. For the burden of carrying around a few lightweight cards in your briefcase, you might make a business connection that will bring in new work and help you keep your job.

The humble business card may be out of vogue in America, but it is still widely used throughout the world as a way of introduction to potential clients. In Asia, businessmen are expected to carry business cards. And they are presented with such ceremony that the exchange is almost elevated to the lofty heights of ritual. Most of the cards are two sided. One side is in the giver's native language and the other in English, so as not to risk losing any opportunity.

American business cards are also changing. There is a psychology behind the look, feel, and design of today's cards. Depending on your industry, your card can be simple and straightforward. One side may contain your name, the company's logo, phone number, e-mail address, and website. But more people are jazzing up their cards, utilizing both sides. On one side might be the company's name and logo, while the other provides your contact information. The idea is that by making the recipient flip over the card, they are more likely to remember you.

The latest trend is a two-sided card with the card owner's photograph. The thinking is that, if flipping a card over helps someone remember you, then adding a photograph will help the card receiver develop more of a connection with you. He or she will remember your face, or your smile, or even your hairdo. In any case, there are some statistics that indicate people do keep business cards with photos on them.

In the old days, people would file their business cards in their Rolodex file on top of their desk. Not anymore. Tech-savvy people usually download the card's information into their Blackberry and computer. What you do with the paper—with or without a photo—is up to you.

It pays to always carry business cards, but especially when you are traveling. You never know whom you are going to sit next to on an airplane or train. You will often find yourself handing out a business card when you least expect it. For instance, Tom recently was taking the train home from a business meeting in Baltimore. He sat next to a well-dressed gentleman on the packed train. Before long, the two struck up a conversation that got around to why they were traveling. The man, it turned out, was a pharmaceutical executive with a well-known company. He asked Tom what he did for a living. Tom responded that he was a business consultant specializing in marketing. The man's face lit up. His department, it turned out, was in the early stages of developing a new marketing plan and was interested in contracting with a consultant. He asked Tom for his card. When Tom got off the train in Philadelphia, the executive said he would be calling. Whether or not anything will come of the encounter remains to be seen. But Tom does know that because he was carrying his business card he just might have found a new client.

27. Get Experience Elsewhere

Experience counts when it comes to keeping your job. But in dour economic times, it's unreasonable to expect anyone at your company to worry about arranging new experiences to make you a better, more versatile employee. Most likely, your manager and the executives above him are too busy fighting to keep the company afloat if business is seriously flagging. Presenting you with a new growth opportunity isn't exactly at the top of anyone's to-do list. Nor should it be.

In good times, your manager may give you more responsibility, maybe even make you the point person on a project. But that still limits you to one project inside your department. In a down cycle, the onus is on you to find new challenges and ways to improve and expand your skills. But you already know that.

So how can you get real, hands-on, senior management experience without being a senior manager? If you are serious about broadening your business vistas, building your career, and reinforcing your brand, there are a couple of ways to do it. Understand up front that you are trading your time and any monetary compensation for exposure to a different, more sophisticated kind of business experience.

The best way to earn serious managerial creditability is to join the board of a high-profile community organization. Many local organizations—charities, community hospitals, private schools, the YMCA, and SPCA—are always seeking to enlist new, talented volunteers. So, for one meeting a month and a few nights a week of prep work, you can gain entrée into the world of senior level management.

When you join a board, have a clear plan about what you wish to accomplish. Don't brag, but do find a subtle way to let your employer know about your new, outside adventure. It will show your boss that you are interested in expanding your horizons and are capable of doing more beyond the scope of your job. Also, if you are serving with any distinguished, influential, or well-known people in the community, it doesn't hurt to discreetly drop a name or two.

Chances are when you join a board you won't vault right into what you want to tackle. That's fine. Treat the organization like a buffet, and sample as many different committees as possible. The idea is to expand beyond the framework of your current paying job, while picking up information and skills that will make you more valuable and help you stay employed.

Most people concentrate only on the career directly in front of them. Joe, however, had a blueprint for his. Part of his plan called for developing new and diverse skills that would not only make him more valuable to his employer but eventually allow him to reach the ranks of senior management. To get the executive management experience he needed, Joe joined the board of a local hospital. It was a nonpaying position, but monetary reward wasn't his goal. He was in it to learn and gather skills that would take him twenty-five years to gain at his company. As a hospital board member, he was exposed to high-level discussions and policy and decision-making.

Joe chose to work on the finance committee, a completely different side of business than his real job. He gained a reputation among other board members, who included CEOs and influential lawyers, for being a quick study and having sound judgment. He also used his board position to develop his skills as an executive coach, working with hospital administrators.

He didn't collect a penny for all the work he did. But now Joe is on a first-name basis with some of the area's most influential business leaders. He has their private telephone numbers and e-mail addresses. How many of his office peers do you think can pick up the telephone and ask the former CEO of a national railroad company for business advice? Probably none. Way to go, Joe.

28. Give Your Manager Your First Impression

Offering your gut reaction during a meeting may not seem politically astute. But being coy when asked for your gut reaction to a new idea may actually put your job in more jeopardy. However you choose to respond is not always a black-and-white issue and will depend on several factors.

Let's say that you are meeting with your manager and colleagues in what is usually a safe environment. Now, let's say that experience tells you that your manager endorses frank discussion and uses these meetings as a way to challenge and enhance new ideas. In that case, feel free to give your gut reaction. Since speaking your mind is encouraged, your silence could be read as disinterest. And when jobs are on the line, you want to be seen as fully engaged.

When your manager asks for a reaction, be the first to jump in with an opinion. Don't hang back and wait for someone else to offer his or her two cents. Being second robs your input of originality. Your thoughts become a secondary support to what the first speaker said, in essence, relegating your position to "me too."

In addition, giving your gut reaction quickly after being asked shows that you have been engaged in the meeting and have strong views on the topic. It tells your manager that you can digest and work through an issue quickly and have the self-confidence to speak your mind, whether you agree with, or challenge aspects of the idea. Those are the qualities of a leader and someone a manager and business want to keep around.

When presenting your gut reaction, start by complimenting the idea's originator. By saying something like "The idea was well thought out," you disarm the person's defenses, making him or her more open to hearing whatever criticisms you have. Then, highlight what you believe is missing from the idea or needs to be improved upon. Always offer a few solutions that respond to your criticisms.

Meetings, however, are not always so open and creative. Sometimes your manager is just listening for a chorus of "amens" from the congregation for his or her new plan. Again, experience should tell you what to expect. If rubber stamping is your manager's idea of input, then stop your gut reaction from reaching your mouth. Unless you have a really, really serious objection and are not worried about the repercussions—like unemployment—don't say a word. If history tells you that the person only wants his or her point of view confirmed, stifle your gut reaction.

There is one catch to that scenario that nullifies your previous experience with your manager. Since business is down and layoffs are probable, the rubber stamp manager may recognize that he will need people who will give him an honest opinion on a plan. He may be trying to smoke out the department's "yes" people. So it might behoove you to offer your gut reaction, even if it is negative. How do you decide what to do? You have to read the situation. Has there been talk about the department or company cutting its ranks? Has money recently shifted away from your division? In other words, does the current business environment invite people to challenge ideas and offer suggestions? If you think it does, then, by all means, speak up. Be engaged in the conversation early so you are seen as someone eager to participate and help. If not, remember, silence is golden and may help you keep your job.

29. Meet with Your Boss Regularly

It is important to have regularly scheduled, face-to-face meetings with your boss when business is humming. But having those meetings when the company is facing downward pressure is absolutely critical. When you are trying to keep your job, the last thing you want to be is anonymous. You want your manager to know you and be familiar with your work.

Even in bad times, regular monthly or quarterly meetings should serve a greater purpose than simply providing an update on what you are doing and your boss's perception of how well you are doing it. Use every encounter to build a relationship with your boss. So don't be afraid to engage in a little small talk before business talk. A manager friend once complained that none of his employees ever asked him how things were going or how his family was doing. So, if you see a picture on the manager's desk of little Sally in her soccer uniform, ask what position she plays or how her team is doing.

When the conversation turns to business, have your discussion points in order. Get the housekeeping issues out of the way as quickly as possible. Be brief, informative, and always positive. Bring your manager up to speed on your current role or project in the department (if either has changed), and your progress. For instance, are you on schedule to meet your deadline? Has the goal changed and, if so, why? Is your budget running over or under? Mention any roadblocks or problems, but don't make this a complaint session.

Your goal at the monthly or quarterly meeting is to get beyond the report-card conversation as quickly as possible so that you can probe your manager on what is happening in the larger landscape. Try to find out how outside influences will affect his decision making and, consequently, your job.

Listening to your manager's world view will give you insight into his or her business priorities. But don't leave that open to interpretation. Ask your manager directly what the department's goals are for the coming month or quarter. Then find out what you can do to help achieve those objectives. Helping your manager succeed is a very good way to keep your job.

DON'T ASSUME

How important is it to meet regularly with your manager? Jeanine Tanner O'Donnell had a client who was ready to leave her job because she was sure her manager was about to fire her. The company had just installed a new order-tracking and processing system that included rather stringent operating guidelines that employees had to follow. O'Donnell's client was having a hard time adjusting and simply couldn't get the hang of the new system. The woman was so sure that her job was in jeopardy that she figured it would be better to leave on her own rather than be fired. She asked O'Donnell to help her update her resume. O'Donnell wondered if the woman had talked to her manager. No, the woman said, she had not, but she was still sure her manager was ready to let her go. O'Donnell suggested that the woman sit down and discuss the situation with her manager. The woman agreed and set up an appointment. During the session, the woman was surprised to learn that, not only was her job safe, but her manager was completely happy with her work. In fact, he thought that she was adapting better than most of his employees to the new system. The moral of the story—don't assume anything. Clear up any questions and concerns by meeting regularly with your manager.

30. Get Feedback on Your Style

Keeping your job requires knowing how well you are performing. Timely, focused feedback allows you to respond quickly and adjust or correct any perceived weakness in your performance. The best way to aquire that depth of feedback is from the people who work with you.

There are several ways you can ask for and receive feedback about your work. Almost every company has regularly scheduled performance reviews with your manager. At most companies, the reviews take place every six months to a year. And it's common, of course, for employees to periodically check in with their managers informally. So, whenever you have a minute with your manager, don't hesitate to talk to him about what he is doing and how the overall project is going.

A really smart employee will follow up those questions by asking for feedback about his own work. By asking your manager for feedback, you are inviting him into a conversation that is sometimes difficult to introduce. Believe it or not, even the best managers find it hard to give an employee feedback, especially if what they have to say is negative. So once you open the door, don't waste your manager's time by asking a general, "So, how do you think I'm doing?" question. You want feedback you can use, so ask your boss about a specific aspect of your work, something real and important, so he can give you a response that you can apply to improve your performance.

Managers rarely are keenly aware or right on top of what are your everyday work endeavors. But the people around you who rely on your contributions to help make the team or project successful do know, and that makes them an important source for feedback. If you have been slacking off, don't bother asking for feedback, because you are not going to like what you hear. But if people know that you are a worker and have played a positive role in the project, their insights will be fair and constructive.

There are a couple of ways to solicit input from your colleagues. For instance, if you are a project or team member, ask individual employees how their work is going. Then, as the conversation moves on, casually slip in what you are doing, and ask if they think that it is helping. Another way is to set up informal meetings with your coworkers that are all about your performance. Colleagues usually won't volunteer information about your job performance. They will, however, tell your manager. You want to intercept and correct any complaints or negative job reviews before your manager hears about it. So bring everyone together, and ask how they think the team is working. Then ask if what you are doing is making everyone's job easier. If it turns out that you are a drag on the project, find out what you can do to improve your performance.

If you favor a more formal evaluation, there are professionally designed surveys available that solicit feedback from a constellation of people—from your manager to outside customers. Most of these 360-degree surveys—so called because they interview everyone around you—are either multiple-choice questionnaires with a one-to-five ranking for each answer, or a questionnaire combined with a written response portion covering each competency.

The questionnaire survey consists of five or more statements about a series of competencies that are then rated by the person answering the survey. In the more detailed survey that includes written answers, the respondent is asked for statements about the individual's strengths and areas where improvement is needed. Both surveys are done anonymously. When completed, the data is compiled and given to the subject so he has an accurate idea of how people view his strengths and weakness.

However you choose to get feedback on your work, bring the data to your performance review with your manager. You will want to show her the feedback you have received and the actions you have taken to address each issue. It is important that your manager have a balanced view of your work.

31. Ask for Recommendations

In some jobs, there is no way to easily quantify your value to the company. But if you want to keep your job, you have to find some way to translate the otherwise hard-to-quantify into rock-solid facts that reinforce the importance of your role in the organization. That is the case with people in the service industry. It is difficult for you to find ways to truly measure your contribution to the company. Nevertheless, you have to devise some method that will show your boss data-based evidence that you are doing your job well and are a part of the company's success.

How do you collect that proof? You can gather the facts by soliciting reviews from your clients or whoever uses your product or services. Once or twice a year, send your clients a note asking them for feedback on your performance. Some customer service people develop a short, easy-to-fill-out, five-question form. Ask them to answer questions like: Are we well informed about the product? Did we provide timely service? Did we follow up to make sure the client was satisfied? Did we understand, and take into account, how the client uses the product to help their customer?

Have your clients rate their answers on a one-to-five scale, with one being the lowest, and five the highest. The survey isn't formal or scientific, but it will give you a tool to start developing a database—the client checking the boxes.

Next, go over your sales records, service calls, invoices, or whatever you use to document your work process. Figure out how much money each of your clients has spent with the company in the last year. Add up the numbers, and then compare the total to your yearly salary. The more your clients spend with the company over and above your salary, the better for your case.

Study your freshly collected information, and write up a summary statement. Make sure you include your salary-to-client expenditure figure. Send it to your manager prior to your performance review. During the review, point out the highlights to your manager, like the percentage of your clients who are very satisfied with your work. In the end, your facts and figures may not be as dazzling as those of someone who has an easily quantifiable job. But when you are fighting to keep your job when everyone else is losing theirs, it is better to have some kind of job record than none at all. Then, if your manager has to make a choice between you and someone who hasn't tried to quantify his or her job, your client satisfaction survey and the salary-to-expenditure comparison may be enough to keep you working.

USE RECOMMENDATIONS TO GET AHEAD

One way to grow and advance inside a company is to ask people with whom you have a good relationship to recommend you to someone for a job. A recommendation from someone influential is a priceless imprimatur.

32. Use Technology to Build Your Career

You don't have to channel your inner geek to use technology as a hedge against losing your job and to build your career. You do need to have a fundamental understanding of computers, and the time, patience, and desire to learn some basic software programs.

When it comes to business applications, Microsoft Office is the standard against which all others are measured. Ask ten business people if they know how to use the software products bundled inside it, and all ten will say yes. And they probably do, if putting information inside of Excel's cells counts. In reality, most people never delve deeper and explore everything Excel has to offer. And that is a pity because Excel is an incredibly powerful business tool for building different styles of charts with varying levels of detail.

Acquiring the knowledge to use everything Microsoft Office and Excel have to offer is not that difficult, and usually free. On its website, Microsoft offers several easy-to-follow videos at no cost. The tutorials are step-by-step lessons that even remind you when to click to save your work. Within a day, even the biggest technophobe can produce a rudimentary spreadsheet. Once you understand Excel, it's on to bigger things, like Microsoft Access, a system that allows you to collect and manipulate report data.

Visio is Microsoft's more advanced and complex computer-aided drawing program. Again, Microsoft has several free tutorials available. Visio gives you the ability to create ultraslick presentations and flow charts by moving and positioning shapes and text.

How will using technology help you keep your job? The easy answer is that it's just one more skill in your arsenal. But the real value comes if you know how to apply that skill to what the company deems important. Don't just tell your manager about your technological competency. Show it off. Put together an amazing presentation using your computer talents. Go in and say, "Ellen, I've been thinking about the new account, and I put together this profile/chart/graph/spreadsheet that shows you how the numbers work out."

Your manager suddenly realizes that you have an unsung talent, and you get to ring up a couple of points on your value-added scoreboard. But you're still not finished. Now tell your manager that you acquired your amazing gift for graphics on your own, working at home late into the dark of night from online tutorials. And there's more. Because you are a great person and a total team player, volunteer to generously share your knowledge with other people in the department. In one meeting, you have shown your manager that you are resourceful and motivated, and that you understand the business.

But you don't want to limit yourself to a single department. If at all possible, use your network to branch out. Let people throughout the company know that you can prepare slick, software-generated presentations and would be happy to do it for them, or teach people in their department. Doing so will lead to introducing yourself and your skills to new people across the company. Then, if things get dire in your department, you may be able find a soft landing in another department inside the company.

FOR THE MORE ADVANCED USER

The creation of social sites such as Facebook, MySpace, LinkedIn, and wikis—websites that allow visitors to add, remove, and edit content—has presented new opportunities for people to expand their computer skills in a way that may help them keep their jobs, like becoming a community manager.

A community manager oversees the operation of an online discussion group or blog, which he or she usually creates. The community manager's job is to make sure the site runs smoothly, is interesting, generates a steady flow of participants, and mediates any disagreements. Sound like the job description of anyone you know?

33. Look for a Mentor

You wouldn't consider summitting Mount Everest without a sherpa, or challenge the Colorado River's white-water rapids without an experienced rafter on board. So why wouldn't you ask someone to guide you through business's vine-tangled jungle during these dangerous economic times? Your life may not be on the line, but your job may well be.

There is no more urgent a time to have a mentor than when business is down. The business equivalent of an advisor, mentors give their less experienced colleagues the benefit of their experience, vision, and professional expertise. They help with your professional development by exposing you to the range of possibilities and options that you might not have considered because you didn't know about them. Mentors are pitchperfect sounding boards for new ideas and dicey decisions. A mentor will not only make you aware of the choppy political waters surrounding you but help you navigate them.

Finding a mentor when everyone is worried about job security is actually easier than you might think. Potential mentors realize that, during tough times, their advice is in high demand. They understand that being a seasoned professional, they can calm a younger, less experienced employee.

Don't be shy about asking someone you respect to be your mentor. The request is, in many ways, the ultimate professional acknowledgment. You can find a mentor inside or outside your company. Outside the company, consider asking a valued teacher or professor. You can tap a more experienced friend, a colleague from another company, someone in your industry, or a family member. The odds of a mentor being helpful go up substantially if he or she works in your industry.

You can find a mentor at almost any level inside the company. Build a personal map of relationships. Let's say you want to move into management. Start drawing your map by writing down the names of all the people inside your company that you respect and who respect you. From that list, choose the people who have the business experience and knowledge you want your mentor to possess. Narrow the list by keeping only the names of people with whom you already have a relationship. Then whittle it down again, this time to the top two people that you feel most comfortable approaching to be your mentor. Remember, this person is going to help you think through critical career decisions.

Invite your mentor candidate out for a cup of coffee, and while she is still stirring, cut to the chase. Say, "Marie, I'd like to ask you a favor. I like my current job, but I want to advance and grow professionally. I don't know if I understand all the ways that I could possibly better myself inside the company. The favor I wanted to ask is, would you consider meeting with me periodically to talk through some of my options and act as my sounding board?" Unless Marie is totally oblivious, she understands that you have just asked her to become your mentor.

BE READY TO TAKE AN OPPORTUNITY

Sometimes a mentor finds you. As a former senior-level manager, Jim Allen says that it wasn't unusual for him to spot a rising young star whom he wanted to help.

"I would ask them, what did they want to do, and they wouldn't have a good answer," says Allen, now vice president of the management consulting firm of Booz Allen Hamilton in McLean, Virginia. "If the boss takes notice and takes an interest and says, 'What are you interested in?' or 'How can I help you?' have a good answer. Make it something that the boss can do, not something crazy."

If you don't have a ready answer, you probably have blown a golden opportunity, the kind that rarely comes around again. If you are lucky and talented enough to be asked the question, be specific about the area you want to work in and the project or team you would like to join. Also, make sure that the position you covet is controlled by the manager, so you know that he can make it happen.

34. Create Your Own Board of Advisers

Having a mentor is great. But why stop there? Why not create your own board of advisers, so that you can have one person guiding you in each specific area of your career?

Having a diverse group of independent voices speaking to you at a time when business is slow, can save your job by giving you different and broader perspectives on the issues confronting your company.

Your board of advisers should be anywhere between three and five members, but no larger than five. Each member should know you and be familiar with your job and the company. Select your board members from people that you trust and respect, because over time you are going to reveal to them a lot about yourself and your ambitions. Finally, make sure that each board member brings something to the table that can add value to your career, whether it is experience, organizational connections, industry recognition, or something else.

So where do you find these people? You probably don't want anyone from your team or department. Having an adviser inside the team can prove tricky. Instead, consider people you know at different levels of the organization and from across the company. These are people who understand what you do and are familiar with the business as you relate to it. Choose people from diverse business backgrounds. For instance, if you are in sales, you might want to draft an advisory board member from marketing. Perhaps another board member could have experience in a different aspect of sales, say, someone who processes what you sell. Next, consider someone from the business side, so that you have a management perspective.

Unlike real business advisory boards, your group will not meet formally. Instead, they will function much more loosely, perhaps as a sounding board for your ideas or to provide a bit of advice on the direction of a project you are working on. If one member gives you a piece of advice, you can always run it past another board member.

Your advisory board plays a prominent role in helping you develop organizational awareness. Ideally, each of your board members works in a different area within the company. Consequently, they each will reflect a different point of view on almost every topic. For you, that means a panorama of perspectives on the same issue. That kind of vantage point is valuable at any time. But when business is contracting, it is absolutely invaluable. You can tell each board member your ideas, and learn what people in their part of the company are thinking, and have a pretty good idea about the kind of support your project will receive, and from whom.

In addition, when you create a board of advisers, you are, in fact, constructing your own little political system. Your board members become your allies, or your coalition. Given that one criterion for choosing each member was experience, each adviser can help you sort out whatever dysfunctional political dynamic is playing out around you. Your advisers can give you a playbook on how to conduct yourself, whom to trust, and how to survive in the company's political environment. Advisory board members can also be great sources of career guidance, telling you what moves you should make, and when you should make them.

35. Relieve Stress

Some stress is good. But study after study has confirmed that unvented job-related stress holds serious implications for the health and well-being of employees. How can relieving stress help you keep your job? The connection is pretty straightforward. If you are feeling stressed, you are likely to be short-tempered with colleagues, make bad decisions, miss crucial deadlines, and miss time at work.

Medical experts have been saying for decades that unrelieved stress can make you seriously ill. A number of studies published in several medical journals over the years have linked job-related stress to increases in blood pressure, inflammation, and anxiety and depression. Researchers have also linked job-related stress to an increased risk of cardiovascular disease, including heart attacks and strokes.

According to the studies, stress can result from a variety of factors, including working too much overtime, having little or no control over job decisions, and the inability of an employee to reposition a job or gain a promotion. Workers who feel the pressure of doing more work and not being given the necessary tools to do the job, are also at risk of developing debilitating stress and depression. Now, on top of all of that, add a slow economy, business downsizing, and personal financial concerns. It is no wonder, then, that people are feeling more anxious and stressed than ever before.

Mental health experts say that men are particularly vulnerable to job-related stress because their identity and social status is more wrapped up in their work. Men are more apt to fret over meeting their boss's expectations, being fired, or wondering what the implications of being passed over for a promotion may mean to their careers. Consequently, they push themselves even harder, because they are afraid of falling farther behind. The greater the psychological strain, the more men feel like they are running on a hamster wheel, and the more likely they will become withdrawn and depressed.

On the other hand, experts say women are more adroit at handling job-related stress. Women generally are more open and willing to talk about their emotions to family members and friends. They volunteer details, including admitting when they are feeling stressed out by their jobs. And unlike men, they will seek help.

The good news for both sexes is that more companies have in-house programs and mental health counselors who can work with employees feeling the strain. There are also stress-reduction training programs that offer strategies for dealing with a difficult time at work.

What can you do on the job? If you have a good relationship with your boss, sit down and explain what you are feeling. Ask him to explain how your job helps the company achieve its goals. Experts say that understanding that your job is important and how it fits into the bigger picture can help improve your feelings of self-worth. But by all means, find someone to talk to. Here are a few more tips on countering the effects of job-related stress.

✔ Don't dwell on what is going wrong at work.
✔ Focus on the things that are being done right.
✔ Talk about what you can do to correct the problem areas.
✔ Adopt a can-do attitude.

GETTING YOUR PRIORITIES IN LINE

Several years ago, Joe Gassman was working on a business deal in Hungary. When quitting time came, Gassman's Hungarian counterpart started packing up to go home. Gassman, who was used to working late every night, asked where she was going. The woman explained that she and her husband had an agreement to only work late on Monday and Thursday nights. Since it was Tuesday, she was going home. Why those nights, he asked?

"She told me that working late on Monday nights gave her a jump on the week," says Gassman, a business projects director for a large insurance company. "Thursday nights gave her the chance to prepare for Friday meetings and to clean up her desk so she could enjoy the weekend. The other nights were spent with her family. It was her way to reduce stress and build a defense mechanism against burnout."

36. Keep Your Job by Staying Physically Fit

You can keep your job by staying in good physical shape. Breaking a sweat lifting weights at the gym; running on the basketball, tennis, or racquetball court; cycling; swimming; jogging; or even taking a brisk walk every day helps energize your body and focus your mind. And working out is probably the best stress buster known to humankind.

Experts say that when you exercise, your body releases a flood of complex chemicals into the bloodstream that helps maintain feelings of self-satisfaction and self-worth. Moreover, a good workout is meditative in that, once you fall into the flow of the activity, your mind becomes singularly centered and everything else slips away. It's not unusual for people to suddenly see the solution to a vexing problem while doing physical activity.

The benefits of regular physical activity include a greatly reduced risk of stroke and cardiovascular disease, carotid artery disease, diabetes, and some cancers. Exercise also increases bone mass, which defends against fractures, and strengthens the immune system. Let's face it, you are not going to keep your job if you are always calling in sick.

Undoubtedly then, the biggest reward for a good workout regimen is keeping your job. With the extra energy and stamina you gain from doing physical activity, you won't wither under the challenge and demand of working more and longer hours as your less fit colleagues. You will also have a healthy attitude and increased self-confidence.

Most of the work and results you will see from getting in shape will happen at the gym. But the work begins in your kitchen. Remember the old computer adage—garbage in, garbage out? Well, you want to do the opposite. It is important to have a healthy diet loaded with fruits and vegetables. Next, find a physical activity that you enjoy doing, be it a sport, just going to the gym to lift weights, watching an aerobics exercise tape at home, or taking a long walk. It's okay to try something different, but whatever you choose, remember, you want to look forward to doing it at least every other day.

If your company has an in-house gym, use it during lunch. One study found that people who worked out during lunch were twenty percent more productive in the afternoon. If you have time to do only one type of workout, make it weight training, because it contains an aerobic component. That's right, weight lifting is a "twofer." Every time you lift a weight—even a bag of groceries— you engage your muscles, which makes your heart beat harder. In turn, that forces the left ventricle—the part of the heart that pumps blood to most of your body—to work harder and become stronger. And just like your biceps, the harder your heart works, the stronger it becomes. And the stronger your heart, the more staying power you have for those long nights at the office.

If overall better condition, a sharper mind, and a healthier heart aren't reward enough, there are some other benefits that might motivate you to start pumping iron. For instance, you can also shed a few pounds. With a thirty-minute session of weight training, the body gets so revved up that it is still burning calories at a supercharged rate two hours after you've grunted the last repetition.

GETTING STARTED

Talk to your doctor and have a complete physical before beginning a workout program. Do weight training every other day, with an aerobic workout on the off days. There are tons of videos, books, websites, and magazines that offer a full spectrum of workouts available. But you can get started with basic exercises like these:

Chest presses or push-ups
Rowing exercise or another type of pulling motion
Leg exercises like squats or leg presses
Core body exercises for the midsection, sit-ups, or crunches

37. Be Deft at Repositioning Your Job

When a company is shrinking because of a slumping economy, be ready to reposition your job. At the first sign of a shift in corporate interest in your department's project, don't shrug it off or hope it will just pass. It makes you look passive and an easy mark when management comes looking for someone to furlough. Rather than lying low and hoping to wait it out, take charge of repositioning your job.

Once you sense your department or team's fortunes are tacking south, start thinking about how you can reposition yourself. Fire up your network and begin repositioning your job. Ask people in your network to introduce you to the influential people in their departments. When you make those contacts, present yourself as a smart, highly versatile, take-charge employee who is anxious to accept new challenges.

All that said, there are some hard-and-fast facts about repositioning your job. The first is, the lower you are in the organization, the more your job and responsibilities are narrowly defined.

If you have a good manager, chances are she will be willing to help you keep your job. If you don't have a cooperative manager, then saving your job just got harder. You probably will be limited to asking for help from your peers and the people in your network. The problem with that is, if they are part of your company or industry, they will be frantically trying to save their own jobs.

If you are lucky enough to be put in touch with people in other areas of the company, you still may be unable to reposition your job. What's left to do? Start relying on yourself. Learn to read and interpret the signs and signals of change, and then develop new ways that you can help your boss weather the storm. If you are a mid-level employee or manager, you have more options and opportunities to market yourself to other departments. Before you do that, however, sit down and talk it over with your manager. Ask her if your sense of what is going on is accurate. If it is, ask whom they would suggest you contact in other departments about transitioning and repositioning your job.

In this frenzy of activity, make it a point to demonstrate to your manager that you are aware of what is going on and are anxious to expand beyond the current parameters of your job. If nothing else, your boss will realize that you are someone willing to learn and develop new skills that fit into the company's recharted course. Management is always looking for people who can see the bigger picture and are willing to stretch themselves to meet new challenges and be part of the solution.

READ THE TEA LEAVES

There are environmental clues that should tip you off that it is time to reposition your job. For instance, if a successful or influential manager is replaced by one who has had a series of failures or has otherwise lost the company's confidence, you can pretty much bet your department/

team/project has fallen off the radar screen and is no longer valued. That is a clear signal that your job is vulnerable and that it is time to reposition yourself.

Also, resources generally flow in the direction of power and influence. If you notice that the department's budget has been cut, it probably means the company is heading in another direction. If you want to maintain your employment status, follow the finances. Why? Think about it. When it comes time to let people go, are the power brokers going to fire workers in the department that the money is migrating to, or the department from where the money was taken? The instant you feel a shift in the financial breezes, get to work repositioning your job.

38. Protect Your Online Image

No one in the corporate world will likely ever admit to scoping out an employee's Facebook or MySpace online page. Nor will a manager ever cite the content of an employee's social site page as the reason for letting him go. But when you are looking for ways to keep your job, why risk it? Police your online image.

Being judged by the images or written content on your Facebook or MySpace page may seem grossly unfair. After all, your online social site is part of your private life and has nothing to do with your job. But in an age where anyone can learn something about everyone, the lines between your private and professional lives has blurred. Indeed, some people argue that accepting a paycheck means you have become a living, breathing symbol of your employer.

The only way to protect yourself, of course, is to scrub clean your online image. Control your little patch of the virtual world by being careful about whom you call or accept as a "friend." The mistake people often make is allowing people they barely know, or a "friend" of a real-life friend, to post on their site. Next thing you know, the new "friend" is posting objectionable photos or writing obscene things on your wall for everyone in your circle to see.

Do not tolerate that. Make it clear to all of your "friends" that you do not want photos of people getting drunk or skinny dipping, because you want to protect your professional integrity online. Anyone who posts that kind of material on your space will be removed from your "friends" list.

People may think you are overreacting. But let's say your manager has just been told that he has to cut his staff and it is between you and another person. After weighing the pros and cons for each person, it's a toss up. Then, by chance, someone who knows your manager and is your online "friend" makes an innocent comment about a lewd photo he saw on your online social site. Whether or not it is fair, whether or not it is a conscious decision, that little piece of information could be the tipping point that costs you your job. So why take the chance that, in some weird, six-degrees-of-separation kind of way, your manager either sees or hears about something on your Facebook or MySpace page that makes him wonder if you are a serious person or a goof-off?

NO SURFING

If you want to keep your job when everyone around you is losing theirs, stop surfing on the Internet at work. When you are at work, do your job. Don't think for an instant your boss or the company doesn't know what you are doing online. Many people still don't realize that once you sign your employment letter, you forfeit your right to privacy. Consequently, the company is free to monitor your every keystroke, from your visits to shopping sites, to the games you play, to every instant message conversation. It is the ultimate in employment "gotcha."

"If I have five employees and I only need three, I can call information technology and ask for each employee's historical performance data and see how much time they really are spending working on the web and playing on the web," says Philip Haynes, managing director of AllianceQ, a corporate recruitment organization in Northbrook, Illinois.

If you really want to keep your job and see your production jump by twenty-five percent, then don't shop online, don't instant message friends during work hours, don't send text messages, accept family calls only in an emergency, and use only forty minutes of your hour lunch break.

39. Get Back into the Game

Every business has "A" players, the hard-charging, work-long-hours go-getters, and "B" players, the solid, hard-working citizens who do their jobs faithfully and well. Companies need both types of employees, even in a down economy. But a company doesn't need, nor will endure during a downshift in business, any employee who isn't contributing as much as she is capable of giving. Call that employee the "S" player, as in self-impressed. "S" employees are nowhere near as good, nor as valuable to the organization, as they think. They are convinced that the company is lucky to have their talent. If that even remotely sounds like you, the only chance you have to save your job is to adjust your attitude and lift your work game to another level.

How you became a legend in your own mind doesn't really matter now. It's time for you to start breathing the air at sea level. To make the dramatic adjustment in attitude that is necessary to get back into the game, you will have to conduct a brutally honest self-assessment. Forget any notion of blaming anyone but yourself for the shortcomings in your career. Be accountable for your lack of contribution to the company, and take full responsibility for your mistakes.

How do you get back in the game? Start by identifying areas where you are deficient. Look for answers in past evaluations and manager comments. Then go over the projects you worked on. Can you learn anything about yourself from the ones that stalled or failed? Now, look at the type of assignments your manager has given you in the last year. Have you been given any real responsibilities? Have you been asked to join a team or get involved in an important project?

Also think about how you treat your colleagues, and how they act toward you. Search for subtle signs like, has anyone recently asked you to go out to lunch? Have you been included when people go out for a drink after work? No? What, then, is it about you that puts people off?

Turn the tables and ask yourself what it is that you do well. Go through the same cycle of questions. After you complete the self-assessment, meet your manager with a plan for raising your game. A couple of cautions here: Don't go into the meeting apologizing for your self-absorbed, low-contribution days. That approach may damage your chance of mending fences, because your manager will immediately think, "So, Sally realizes that with the bad economy, jobs are on the line, and now she wants to get in my good graces." Your manager may politely listen to you, but she won't be supportive.

Another reason not to be apologetic or mention your black sheep days is that your manager knows all too well that you have been a drag on her department. So why bring it up? Instead, go in and say something like, "I realize that these are challenging times for you and the department, and I want to help. Here are some things I've been thinking about doing to increase my contribution." Being positive and proactive shows your manager that you are aware of the dire situation, know and accept your reputation, and are ready to be a team player. Your manager will appreciate that you are quietly acknowledging the sins of your past and want to pull your weight by coming up with ideas.

Finally, your rehabilitation has to be sincere. People will be watching to see if the leopard really has changed its spots. Your manager and coworkers will want to see that you are in it for the long term and not just reacting to economic circumstances and job security. Your coworkers want to see your game rise to a higher level and stay there. Who knows, an "A" player may even ask you out to lunch.

Part II

Keep Your Job
by Helping Others

We are never better as human beings than when we are self-lessly helping someone else. By its nature, creating your brand requires you to concentrate on different ways to keep your job by doing things by yourself and for yourself. And that is fine, smart, and necessary for anyone who wants to stay employed and advance his or her career. After all, if you are not willing to invest the time and the sweat equity for your own success, why should a manager or company do so?

But can lending a helping hand to someone else really help you keep your job? At a time when people are losing their jobs, you bet it can, and in several ways. By extending yourself to help a colleague, you show everyone who you are as a person, not just as a coworker. People understand that you see over the horizon, well beyond your job. They know they can trust you. And as we already know, trust leads to respect.

As for your managers, they see the same thing, and more. They see someone who, even in the most dire employment cir-cumstances, is self-confident and the ultimate team player. But they also see the mark of a leader in your actions.

You have probably, at some time, experienced the satisfac-tion that comes with knowing that you consciously set a goal, thought through and carefully planned how you were going to attack the goal, dedicated a serious portion of your life to achiev-ing the goal, and finally, one day, basked in the success and accomplishment of realizing the goal.

But even that can't match the unique satisfaction you feel when you lend a hand to help a new person get acclimated to your company, or make sure the credit for a job well done is shared by everyone, or when you play a role in advancing, or saving, someone's career. Each time you lend a helping hand to your colleagues, you are transforming your company from a business to a team. And if you are really lucky, the people on that team may one day feel like they are all family.

The head of your department's family is the manager. When business turns cold, the burden for helping the company survive falls squarely on your manager's shoulders. While your manager always wants her department to run like a well-oiled, highly productive, seamless operation, there is a new, palpable urgency when the economy is slipping into recession. She is expected to invent ways to motivate a shrinking workforce to produce more with less, while still handling the day-to-day task of managing. And every day the load gets heavier.

Jeff Kaye, president and CEO of Kaye/Bassman, a Plano, Texas, search firm, says that when the bottom falls out of the economy, managers have to carry more and more of the load. He likens your manager to someone carrying a load of bricks on her back while trying to move forward. Every time someone gives your manager a new task, it is like adding another brick to the load. If you want to keep your job, Kaye says, offer to remove and carry some of the bricks from your manager's load. That is how you become an asset to your boss.

There are all shapes and sizes of "bricks" you can remove from your manager's back. In each case, it is just a matter of you stepping up and offering to help. You can take a brick away by simply backing your boss and supporting her decisions, even if you don't agree. Or maybe you want to eliminate a series of bricks by helping your manager develop a series of policies affecting everything from stamping out gossip in your office, to creating a worst-case disaster plan.

One of the easiest bricks to remove from your manager's load is completely within your control. Once you recognize that change is coming, accept it. Control your anxiety, and become part of the force working for change. Do that, and your manager's load will become feather light.

40. Let People Know You Enjoy Your Job

When business goes sour, morale suffers. Employees start worrying about losing their jobs. People start pointing fingers and second-guessing management's every decision. Rumors spread like fire in a lumber yard. It's hard to blame people who are scared. But now is not the time for you to join the Greek chorus of doom and gloom. It may sound counterintuitive, but put on a happy face. Be upbeat, but not in a syrupy or Pollyanna way. Show people that you love your job, want to keep it, and want to help turn things around. Let people know that you believe in the company by being interested, even enthusiastic, about every project that you are assigned.

It doesn't take that much effort to show people how much you enjoy your job. It really is pretty basic. Start by being cordial with your colleagues. Say hello to people you meet in the hallway, even if you don't know them. Ask folks how their day is going. Engage them in conversations about their kids, their vacation, the local sports teams, the latest movie they went to see. If you smile and laugh, people will automatically assume that you enjoy what you are doing.

There are plenty of other ways to show people that you like your job. For instance, when you go for a cup of coffee, ask if you can get one for someone else. And if you drain the last cup, take a minute to brew a fresh pot. Never leave your dirty dishes in the sink for someone else to clean. When the day is over, make an effort to say goodnight to your coworkers. If any of those suggestions sound familiar, it's because they echo what your mother told you about being polite. By the way, she was also right about eating all your vegetables.

You can also convey job satisfaction by participating in group endeavors, whether it is joining a work project, playing on the company softball team, or organizing an outing. And what's the big deal about singing a few rousing choruses of happy birthday and having a piece of pound cake a couple of times a year? In fact, if your office mates invite you to do something together, and your social calendar is clear, what advantage is there in turning them down?

OPEN-DOOR POLICY

Joe Fenico is an ardent practitioner of showing his coworkers how much he loves his job. As a human resources manager, Fenico walks through the office every day saying hello to employees and asking if there is anything he can do for them. But to him, the real proof that he loves his job is that his office door is usually open.

"What makes me valuable to people is if they feel that they can come to me and trust me," he says. "I'm a positive person and I am sure that whatever success I have had over the years it is because of my style."

41. Be Civil to Your Colleagues

Practice the "Golden Rule": Treat others with the same dignity, respect, and civility that you want and expect. Approach your job and your colleagues in a positive, trusting manner. Look for the best in others and believe that they are doing their best to be their best.

What's that you say? The Golden Rule is a beautiful tenet for living your life, but we're talking hardcore, no-holds-barred business here, capitalism gone wild. Well, with apologies to the old advertising slogan "Try it. You might like it," your brand should exemplify civility, if for no other reason then it is simply the right thing to do. In business, civility is the pathway to respect. And earning the respect of your coworkers can pave smooth the road to success. How? Because no matter what we achieve in business, it requires the help and cooperation of other people. The greater your accomplishments, the more trust and respect you earn from your fellow workers. Just remember that the key to earning that respect is civility.

Being civil does not mean being nice, not that you shouldn't also be nice. The words are not synonymous. Being civil insists that you always treat people politely and courteously. That goes double for the people you don't like. The business definition of civil also means that you always try to do the right thing.

When your brand includes civility you will find that people are more willing to share their knowledge, ideas, and insights with you. They are more open because they respect you and know that you respect their views. The additional information you glean from your colleagues' input can help you make better, more informed judgments and decisions, which will enhance your opportunity of becoming a leader. But how can civility help you if the other person isn't reciprocating? Simply do your best and never stoop to their level. Let's assume that an individual's actions appear to be running counter to what you are trying to do. How do you handle it? You assume that the other person is driven by the same thing that motivates you, wanting to do what is best for the business. By assuming that is also what your counterpart wants, you create a common ground and a foundation for that person to trust you. So, simply believing that the other person is motivated by good changes the situation's dynamic, which, in turn, may change the person's behavior.

Even if it doesn't sway the other person, your colleagues will know that you were civil and treated the person fairly, which, in the end, will increase their respect for you.

CIVILITY IN ACTION

As a senior department manager, Fran Landolf faced a situation when a colleague tried to divide his staff. The manager told employees that Landolf wasn't interested in their work. One employee approached Landolf and asked if that was true. Landolf said it wasn't, and then called the other manager. He explained to the manager that he did value the work being done and hoped that the manager would pass along the message.

"I said, you know these guys and they respect you. I want you to know how I feel so you can tell them," says Landolf, now a Baltimore, Maryland, executive coach and business consultant. "He may not have liked that I called him on it in a way that wasn't confrontational. But it totally disarmed him from ever going to that group again and telling them how I felt about their work. My guess is his respect for me increased, and the respect for me from the other guys probably went up as well."

42. Respect Experience

Getting along with coworkers is necessary if you want to keep your job. But your ability to work well with older employees will definitely help you keep your job.

Business is in the midst of one of the biggest workforce demographic shifts in American history. Older workers, many of whom have spent their entire careers in one industry, will slowly be leaving the workforce over the next decade, taking with them a library's worth of company and industry knowledge. Be smart and avail yourself of that ton of knowledge just itching to be passed on.

How can you tap into that information? That's easy enough. Just show respect for your colleague's years of dedication to her profession. Ask questions about how the company or industry has evolved. Show an interest in her experiences, and listen to her take on how change has affected the work. An experienced employee may also make a great formal or informal mentor.

The "generation gap" is such a sixties concept. Nevertheless, a separation between younger and older employees does exist, particularly when it comes to computers and technology. While technology is all but innate to many younger employees, older coworkers, like your baby boomer colleagues, know how to use a computer. But chances are they aren't as nimble at getting around the Internet as you. So, if you see an older colleague struggling with technology, see it as an opportunity to help. Ross Mayfield, founder of Socialtext, a company that creates corporate wikis (websites that allow visitors to add, remove, and edit content), tells the story of an older CEO who never touches a computer keyboard but is still his company's top blogger. How does he do it? His assistant. Mayfield says the CEO either scribbles down his thoughts on paper or dictates his blog to his dutiful assistant, which she then types and posts. As for the comments, she prints them for him to read.

Going out of your way to bridge the technology gap will earn you goodwill points with your manager, which can help you keep your job.

SAVING VALUABLE KNOWLEDGE

Back when Dave started as the police reporter at the local newspaper, the county was mostly farmland. But over the years, the countryside slowly changed until the transition from farming to bustling suburb was complete. All the while, Dave faithfully covered his beat, getting to know a succession of local police and fire chiefs who in turn introduced him to town council members, business people, county commissioners, and congressional representatives. He always asked for their cards or phone numbers. His Rolodex was bursting with the names of everyone who knew someone in the county and beyond.

Dave was willing to share his sources. If a fellow reporter needed someone to talk to about a story, Dave would start flipping through his Rolodex until he found the right source.

"Just tell them we work together and that I said that it was okay to talk to you," he would instruct the reporter.

As Dave got older, he seldom left his desk. Still, he managed to get the story, including details other reporters at the scene either missed or were not given. Then, during a budget crisis one year, word came down that each department would have to let one person go. Everyone in the newsroom thought Dave, who was closing in on retirement, would be sacrificed. But he wasn't. The editor instead chose the paper's newest reporter. When asked later how he made his choice, the editor said it was easy.

"Dave knows more about this county than anyone," the editor said. "Plus, no one has better connections and is willing to share them. A newspaper depends on a good network of sources. We couldn't afford to lose someone like Dave."

43. Be a Team Player

If you're looking for an example of what it takes to be a great team player, study the athletes on successful sports franchises. Good teams have great players who want more than to pad their individual statistics. As teammates, they understand that to become a dominant team every player must enjoy a measure of success. So, instead of grabbing the glory of scoring the winning basket, run, or goal, they set up a teammate. And you know what? The player who scores will almost every time, in some way, form, or fashion, publicly acknowledge the player who assisted.

The same principle applies in business. If you want your team to realize its goal, help your teammates succeed. If you are a senior member of a team, have the credibility and earned the respect of your teammates, your job is to transfer your knowledge and expertise to your teammates. You can do that by providing positive, encouraging feedback. When things are going well, be generous with praise. Go out of your way to tell people that they are doing a good job. The same holds true if a teammate needs a course correction. Be there to offer the advice and support he needs to get back on track.

Being a team player is even more important when things are not going well. Members of high performing teams know that when times are tough they must lift each other's spirits and lighten the mood. During down times, teams need stability and a safe place to regroup. As a teammate, you can provide that steady hand by doing the little things, like bringing in donuts a few mornings, or getting your manager to spring for pizza at lunch. The idea is to create a sense that the team will get through the bad times together. Again, when the best professional sports teams are losing, there is always someone in the dugout, on the bench, or in the locker room, saying positive things to encourage and lift her teammates' spirits.

What do you get out of being a great team player? There is something very powerful about watching individual members of your team coming into their own and knowing that you helped them. It is equally satisfying to see your team bond as you all work toward your singular goal. The more cohesive and productive your team is, the more your credibility and leadership stock rises. Your manager will see in you·the kind of selfless leader he wants working for him.

GOING FROM TEAM JERK TO TEAM PLAYER

Every office has a jerk, and when things get economically tight, you know who is going to feel the sharp edge of the blade first. If you are the jerk, it's time to change your ways. Say one day, you have an epiphany and suddenly want to become the rah-rahiest of team players. Regardless of your sincerity, people aren't going to buy the idea that you changed overnight. And they shouldn't, because the transition from jerk to teammate takes time and a lot of crow eating.

To pass the sincerity test, you have to ask for feedback from your peers. And then, you have to genuinely thank everyone after they tell you that you're a jerk. Next, you have to apply the feedback you received to correct your behavior. People will be watching, so don't try any shortcuts. To be fully redeemed, you must show a real interest and effort in helping other people succeed. As people begin to trust that you are sincere, humble, and not self-serving, they will respond. But your teammates will continue to look for consistency and authenticity in your behavior to make sure you're not trying to fool anyone.

44. Give Your Colleagues Credit

There is nothing easier to do, that pays so much in dividends, as making sure that your colleagues get their share of the credit for the success of a project. When you spread the credit among your coworkers for a winning project, it actually casts you in a positive light. By deflecting credit onto others, you gain in status and prestige, two very important ingredients in the formula for keeping your job.

Recognizing each person's contribution to a job/project/company is really what team-building is all about. It's not just about the person who pushed the ball over the goal line. It's as much about the teammate who designed the play and the guy who ran interference that allowed the ball carrier to score. And who coordinated the execution of the plan? The team leader.

People respond to good leaders who bend over backwards to make sure their people get their share of the credit. Before long, people will ask to work with you because they know that you are not a self-promoter. They know that when you make the presentation you will acknowledge and credit the group's work and what it accomplished. So simply by virtue of sharing the credit with your coworkers, some of it washes back on you.

Yet plenty of people still don't understand the meaning of the old saying, "There is no 'I' in Team." They are consumed with showing everyone what they can accomplish on their own. They are afraid that if they aren't getting all the credit, they are somehow less valuable to the organization. The fact is, when it comes to a team project, your manager and your manager's manager didn't rocket from the mail room to the board room with no stops in between. They know that 99.9 percent of the time, a project's outcome isn't the doing of one very industrious person. Sure, one person does the presentation, but they know that there were ten people behind the scenes contributing information, helping hammer out solutions, and writing the final report and its conclusions.

They know this because not so very long ago they were on a team similar to yours. Moreover, if you use "I" all the time, you are risking a whisper rebellion by your teammates. Word will spread across the company that you are a jerk who takes credit for other people's work. That one comment will spread across the company like a virus and ruin your brand and maybe your job.

TAKE NOTE OF YOUR TEAMMATES

It is not unusual to be the leader of a team that includes senior-level executives. So if you get tapped to head up a project, take careful note of precisely who is seated around the conference table. Obviously, you don't want to favor anyone on your team. Nevertheless, be mindful of how you talk to, and act toward, your teammates. You can bet that they are closely observing your leadership performance. For better or worse, they will remember how you acted under pressure. But most importantly, they will be watching to see how generous you are when it comes to doling out credit for the work. The last thing you want are a couple of executives telling their peers that they would steer clear of you at all costs and never allow you on one of their projects.

45. Draw Attention to a Colleague's Good Work

Giving credit to your teammates is important. But when you turn the spotlight on a coworker who is doing a good job, even if you are not part of the project, the brightness also reflects well on you with management.

Now, to get Prius-type highway miles from your otherwise selfless act, go the next step. Suggest to your manager the institution of an informal employee recognition award, which, by the way, you would be happy to create and oversee.

Volunteering to develop an employee award system works on multiple levels to help you keep your job. First, it shows that you care about your colleagues, registering points in the team player category. And willingly showering attention and praise on your coworkers shows your manager that you are self-confident.

Senior managers view your effort to build an employee reward program as the work of someone who is investing in the company's future by finding ways to retain good people. At the same time, the program you have established helps you stand out with your manager; it also makes him look good to the people above. Finally, your leadership qualities, initiative, and creativity make you the kind of employee a company doesn't want to lose.

The reward program doesn't have to be elaborate. Ask your manager to describe the exact type of recognition program he envisions and what kinds of awards he is willing to give to employees performing outstanding work. Perhaps someone who has spent months and countless hours dedicated to a project that has been successfully completed might receive a day off. If that isn't practical, then maybe the employee can enjoy an extended lunch hour. For those special moments when an employee lands a big contract or completes a tough project, your manager should round up department employees and publicly acknowledge the individual's accomplishment. The token of gratitude—say a day off—would then be announced.

Another reward might be having the key senior staff members sign a memo recognizing the individual's work. Knowing that your boss's bosses are aware of who is doing what in your department is a tremendously effective, not to mention cheap, motivational tool. Too often, employees are left in the dark about what senior managers know or don't know concerning their contributions. A letter or memo handed to the recipient in front of colleagues tells everyone that his work matters to the people several rungs up the ladder.

The program can even be geared to people who aren't home-run hitters, but who still consistently do the everyday little things right. Your manager might acknowledge the efforts of these steady but non-game-changing workers with cards that say something like, "Good Job," or "Thanks for Your Effort." Personalize each card by writing in the employee's name, along with what it is that he does right. Instead of holding a public ceremony, your manager could simply walk up to an employee's desk and hand her a card, with a reminder to bring it to the next performanace evaluation.

46. Support Your Boss

When business is in a downturn, a smart way to keep your job is by making your manager's workload lighter. With less manpower, more bad projects are bound to land on your manager's already brimming plate. So why not pitch in and earn some job-inoculating gratitude?

Just like you, your manager has things she doesn't like to do. For example, a particular task may be the proverbial last straw for your manager. Or it may eat up too much of her time, or require way too much effort—or she may simply not enjoy doing it. That's the time for you to step up and make the problem vanish. Say, for example, your manager isn't good at making Microsoft Excel spreadsheets. You, on the other hand, are an Microsoft Excel savant. Spreadsheets are right in your creative wheelhouse. So, you might most magnanimously say, "Hey boss, let me take care of that for you because I want to help you out."

You have just entered the realm of win/win. You have removed a really irritating job from your manager's "Must Do" list. She is now free to focus on things she wants to do, and thus do well. Plus, you are going to let your manager have all the credit. That's right; you don't want any credit, at least not officially.

Many employees don't recognize the inherent benefit of supporting the manager. But then again, most workers have no idea what their manager is trying to accomplish within her own career. All you need to do is ask your manager a few questions, like: What are your goals? What are your career visions? What do you want to accomplish? If your interest hasn't shocked your manager, nudge her further by asking what you or your team can do to help. Then wait a few moments until she regains the ability to speak.

But seriously, if you think about it, supporting your manager and her career goals makes sense. After all, by helping her get where she wants to go, the chances of you going along are pretty darn good. Why? Because managers aren't dumb. A good manager can identify a smart employee right away. She also knows that without your help and hard work, she may move forward in her career, but at a much slower pace. Supporting and being an asset to your boss by offering to help out means she will begin to see you as someone critical to her advancement and career satisfaction. Your manager will begin to depend on you to produce good work in the clutch. And once your manager begins to feel that you have her back, your mere presence relieves some of her stress. As an employee trying to save your job, you want to deliver either production performance or stress relief to your manager. If you can deliver both, your job is bank-vault safe.

Mike Matthews learned about that when he offered support to his manager, the regional vice president of Baltimore Stanton Chase International. The vice president was charged by the company to produce a quarterly newsletter for clients. It was a thankless, time-consuming job, not to mention a logistical nightmare. The newsletter editor had to find people to write the articles and make their deadlines. Then the stories had to be edited, laid out, and sent to the printer.

Seeing an opportunity to support the vice president, Matthews offered to ride herd on the newsletter for him. Matthews did all the work, making sure the newsletter got written, edited, and sent out on a regular basis. But at the company's global meeting, the regional vice president took all the credit for producing the newsletter. Matthews didn't mind. He knew how these things worked. And anyway, he took on the project to help out his boss. Well, when the regional vice president got promoted to chairman, he remembered Matthews's work. Today, Matthews is the North American regional vice president. Just remember, a rising tide lifts all boats.

47. Support Your Boss's Decisions

At some point in every employee's career, he has sat in a department meeting listening to the manager lay out the company's newest strategy for success during good times. And as he listens, all the employee can think is, "This is a stupid idea. It's just the latest fad that will last six weeks before the next latest-and-greatest idea comes along, and we try that." Now, just imagine the kind of harebrained schemes that arise when business is tumbling downward.

Still, no matter how profoundly dumb you think a plan may be, if you want to keep your job, make the smart play and get behind your boss. You can certainly voice your opinion. In fact, disagree all you want, and as vehemently as you want. Tell your boss as plainly as you like why you think the plan is flawed. Outline every shortcoming that you see in it. Detail each pitfall you envision. But do it behind closed doors. And once the boss says, "This is the plan we're going with," jump on board.

When you walk out of that conference room, your job is to support your manager's decision. In public, endorse the plan like it was your idea. Let colleagues know that you intend to put your oar in the water and pull hard on behalf of the new plan. Be prepared for a backlash. Others attending the same meeting who also believe the new strategy is a loser, may think that you are untrustworthy and are just trying to curry favor with the boss. Who cares. Those people don't understand that, in reality, all you are doing is trying to help the company be successful, while carefully managing your career. And you should be doing both. Good managers want employees who are capable of making tough decisions with an eye toward their career.

So, if you start hearing people talk about you behind your back, grow a thicker layer of skin and move on. Look, what good would you accomplish by being negative or openly challenging the company's decision to head in a new direction? If the business's bottom line is already suffering, creating turmoil and disruption by opposing your manager's plan will only make things worse. Plus, publicly undercutting your manager will make you a juicy target for firing.

On the flip side, by supporting his decision, your manager will view you as a team player. But even more importantly, you will retain your seat at the table. And that is vital because if the new plan fizzles, you will be positioned to suggest ways to recraft the plan, or offer your own plan.

So the choice is yours. If you buck your manager's agenda, he will most likely replace you, or, at the least, move you to a position with less influence. But perhaps more to the point, when you don't support your manager, you are seen as a person who is undependable and has helped undermine a serious decision. If you support your manager, you will be viewed as loyal, trustworthy, and a hard worker. Which of those two employees do you think your manager will want to keep on the payroll?

MAKE SMART BUSINESS DECISIONS

Always publicly support your boss. Doing so, however, does not mean that you should go down in flames with her. Part of career building is developing good business sense and sound judgment. If it is clear that your manager is losing the support of senior management, it is time for you to make a business decision about your future. Depending on how rapidly the sands are sliding through the hourglass, moving to another position or department may be a matter of self-preservation. You don't have to bad-mouth her, or in any way be disloyal. In fact, you shouldn't. You just want to make sure that if your boss is going down, you don't want your job and career to be part of the collateral damage.

48. Allow Your Manager to Take Credit for Your Idea

Let your manager take credit for your idea. It's a smart move for three reasons. First, no matter how much he brags about his new concept, he ultimately knows the real source—you. Plus, the chances of your idea being implemented go way up if your manager is invested. And finally, it's a savvy way to keep your job.

Part of your job is to help your boss be successful, especially if you like working for him. But employees sometimes forget that their boss also has a boss or bosses whom he reports to and from whom he receives a semi-annual or annual job performance evaluation. Like you, your manager has to document everything his department has accomplished, whether or not the department has reached its prescribed goals, and what amount of revenue it has generated or money it has saved. In essence, your manager's job performance evaluation is really based on a magnification of how well you and your coworkers have performed your jobs. When seen through that prism, a manager taking credit for an idea or two doesn't seem like such a big deal.

Letting your boss take credit for your idea may actually be in your best interest, especially when business is down. Let's say you have a good solution to a problem but you know that with the way things are in the company right now, new ideas aren't going to get very far. You know that you don't have the influence to maneuver around the system. But your manager may have the necessary muscle. Sure, you would like the credit, but that's not as important as having your idea implemented. Chances are if you go into your manager's office and say, "I've got this idea and here's how I think we should implement it," it won't get off the ground.

The better way to approach it is to slowly, over weeks, introduce your idea by mentioning different aspects of it when you are talking to your manager. Then, when the time seems right, present this great idea that the two of you have been talking about for weeks. Once your manager is invested, he will carry the ball forward.

Another way to bring your idea to life is by piggybacking onto another project. For example, the business manager of a medical practice at a city hospital wanted to expand his group's services to the suburbs. When he heard about the hospital's plan to open a diabetes testing center, he saw an opportunity.

He invited the administrator planning the diabetes center to lunch. Over their meal, the business manager showed the hospital administrator surveys and other statistics that showed strong patient support for hospital-sponsored medical specialty suburban offices. The hospital administrator looked at the information but said the current plan was only for a diabetes testing center. The business manager smiled and changed the conversation.

A few weeks later, the hospital announced that it had revised its plan and was instead taking the innovative step of building a facility that would house several medical specialty practices, as well as the diabetes testing center. Nowhere did the release credit the business manager for the idea. Sometimes it is more important that you get something done than get credit for an idea that never gets done.

49. Lead the Continuing Education Program

There are lots of ways to get an education inside an organization. You learn the basics from your manager, who teaches you the job. As you gain experience, you move from project to project, and team to team, picking up new skills with each job. Along the way, your responsibilities expand, and you are given the task of initiating a project, or bringing one to a close. Before long, you even know where in the organization to look for your next challenge.

In order to meet those challenges and to continue growing and moving up the organization's ranks, you need to continually upgrade and improve your skills, as you already know from Tip 15: Build Skills for Job Security. Since you are already seeing to your own educational needs, why not compound the effect by becoming the person who helps other employees keep their training and certifications current?

You can probably get the job of overseeing continuing education by simply asking your manager to get you involved. Say something like, "Denise, I'm interested in continuing education and would like to support the department and company by keeping track of the programs available to our employees." If necessary, suggest that your involvement could benefit your manager, by adding that employees versed in the latest techniques produce more in less time, which will make her a contender for manager of the year.

Once the manager gives you the green light, meet with your coworkers to find out what types of classes and testing they are now involved with. You want to get as many of your colleagues as possible invested in creating a continuing education program. So ask for their ideas about the kind of classes, seminars, and conventions they would like to see added to the program. But make it clear that, with money tight, the company may not be able to afford to send people to all the classes, seminars, or conventions.

Part of your job as the leader of continuing education is to compare your program with those of other companies in your industry. What classes, seminars, and conventions do your chief competitors require for employees? Then, go to industry associations and organizations to find out what tests and training are required to maintain certifications.

You may also offer your coworkers tutorials to prepare them for upcoming tests. Offer to give them a compact disc containing the related test information, so that they can play it on their way to and from work, rather than during office hours. If you know the company is about to undergo change, you can get ahead of the curve by organizing training sessions long before the transformation begins. Also, try to bring in outside speakers to speak to your colleagues, and look for new, cutting-edge programs that may improve worker production.

A portion of your job will be dedicated to keeping track of who is taking what class, where the class is being held, how long the class runs, and how expensive it is. Remember, money is tight, so quantify the value for your manager. Break down, in dollars and cents, the value of sending people to a class, against the value to the company of what they learn. One way to get a bigger bang for the buck is to cut back the number of people attending the same convention. For instance, if you normally send five people, reduce it to two. Upon their return, the two employees chosen to attend must file a report with your manager. They will also be required to give a presentation to their colleagues. And the thrust of that presentation has to be insight into action; that is, how the department can implement what they learned.

Being the continuing-education czar will require a lot of work and a lot more patience, especially when people forget their special test code or identification number. Still, you will probably reap a great deal of satisfaction knowing that, as you fight to keep your job, you are also helping colleagues keep theirs.

50. Start a Professional Organization Inside Your Company

No matter where you work inside a company, you can show the initiative and creative leadership necessary to help you build your career. It's true that it may be more challenging to get noticed from some jobs than other, higher profile positions. It's also true that some people have a knack for knowing how to showcase their business talent. But sometimes all it takes is some old-fashioned desire to simply want more.

Take Carol, for instance. An executive assistant, Carol was interested in learning more about her profession and developing relationships among her peers at the company. So she decided to host an informal monthly meeting and invite everyone in the company's secretarial staff to come and talk about how they each did their jobs. The first meeting drew twelve of Carol's colleagues. But it wasn't long before thirty assistants were attending. In fact, the meetings were so popular that Carol bumped them up to twice-monthly, one-hour lunch meetings with full agendas. At these meetings men and women from throughout the company share tips with each other about what they do well, and how they do it.

Today, Carol has earned the status and respect of a leader. She is regarded company-wide as the spokesperson for all of the executive assistants. Moreover, she and her group have created a higher set of standards for executive assistants and raised the group's level of professionalism. By showing some initiative, Carol was able to create an organization that not only serves the needs of the executive assistants but benefits the company. Her efforts have raised her profile inside the company and, in so doing, help protect her job.

Too often, however, people believe that they are stuck in one place with no options and no hope. Consequently, they develop an entrenched "us versus them" mindset when it comes to the company, leading to an attitude of, if you don't pay me to do something, than I am not going to do it. What they don't realize is that people who want to advance don't worry about being paid to go the extra mile, especially when the economy is shaky and people are trying to protect their jobs. But employees who feel forgotten or who are otherwise not invested in the company, simply don't care. And while that is a shame, it is understandable. When you are already working long, hard hours and don't see a way to advance, it's hard to think about giving an extra, free contribution. So stop thinking that it's free. Instead, consider it your chance to jump off the treadmill to nowhere, move your career forward, and keep your job. Why should you expect anyone to invest in you if you are not willing to invest in yourself? No one asked Carol to bring the assistants together. But she did, because she wanted to learn. And her desire to be more, to do more has benefited everyone—the company, the assistants, and yes, Carol.

If you want to keep your job and advance your career, don't sit back and hope that someone else will do it for you. Tomorrow, look across the lunch table at your colleagues who are performing the same work as you. You can bet there is a Carol or two among the group. And right now they are doing something to be ready to take advantage when the next opportunity comes along. The question is, are you doing anything right now that will make your manager want to give you a shot at the next opportunity? Remember, it is your career. It is your life. It is your choice.

51. Create a Glossary of Office Terms

At one time or another, almost everyone has found themselves in a meeting where a businessperson from outside the organization is delivering a speech that sounds like she is casually dropping in words and phrases from a concocted language. Well, she is. You see, she is speaking in the newly minted dialect of her business, department, or team.

Now, just think of how a new member of your team reacts the first time your group starts jabbering in your local business dialect. Lost, right? Well, you can help your new coworker by creating and giving him a glossary of the department's insider terms. It may not seem like much, but the new kid in the meeting will thank you. So will your manager because she won't have to stop and explain the meaning of that odd-sounding random group of letters masquerading as a word, every time the new employee looks puzzled. And any time you make your manager's job a little easier, the more she likes you, and the better your chances of keeping your job.

So how did business-speak get so out of hand? Prior to 2000 and the big Y2K scare, business jargon was pretty tame and easy to decipher. It was rooted in word combinations that offered at least a glimmer of the real meaning of the two words. With just a little effort, you could figure out what terms like *outsourcing, core competencies, right-sizing,* and *speaking offline* were suggesting.

But after Y2K, workplace jargon bloomed like algae in a nutrient-rich pond. Today, business is lousy with letters forged together to pass for words. Take, for instance, the algebraic-like business formula RA2 Interface. Today, we have business terms like: "best of breed," obviously inspired by the American Kennel Club, and "visualized front-end solutions," which sounds more like a marriage of psychology and heavy moving equipment. And lately there has been more "drilling down" in the board rooms of America than in the oil fields of Saudi Arabia. If that isn't enough, there are the acronyms, abbreviations, and symbols used in e-mail, instant messages, and text messaging. It's a wonder the new people joining your group don't need footnotes to read a message or listen to a speech.

The truth is, your group and others throughout business have developed the special terminology as a shorthand for otherwise complicated ideas. And that's fine, except it puts new people and those from outside your organization at a disadvantage. Ultimately, it can slow down the entire process. That is where your glossary comes into play. Take the time to write down every department-specific acronym, along with its full meaning. Then define technical terms, abbreviations, and other jargon frequently used by your group. Suggest to your manager that, as a courtesy to a new employee or a guest attending a meeting, people using office-speak explain the full meaning.

The glossary should be regularly updated and included in every orientation pack. Finally, ask everyone in the department to help a new employee get the hang of the language. As with anyone learning the dialect of a foreign language, once the new kid gets totally immersed in the culture, they too will be drilling down to reach the granularity of the interface product with the best of their colleagues.

52. Be a Mentor

Being a mentor is a great way to help your colleagues, and keep your job. To mentor someone, you must first be successful and proven at your job. Also, people in your office, including your manager, must see you as credible and respect your industry experience and business acumen.

Let's say you have all those things going for you. How do you find an acolyte? You can't just hang out a "Mentor for Hire" shingle on your desk. You don't find them; they find you. What you can do is position yourself. For instance, you could informally bump into someone you think could use your help and strike up a conversation. At some point during your chit chat, you casually let it drop that, "If there is anyway I can help you, feel free to give me a call, or better yet, come see me." The person may not take you up on your offer, but he may mention it to someone else. Mentoring, it turns out, is a word-of-mouth enterprise.

Another place to find someone to mentor is among your project teammates. Let your colleagues know that you are available to work with anyone who would like some guidance. Tactfully say at a team meeting something like, "Hey, if anyone needs help, just give me a buzz." Say it loud enough so everyone in the room hears it.

Follow up by showing an interest in each person's work. Drop by a coworker's desk, where he feels most comfortable and is more likely to ask for help. Then, for example, if someone is doing an invoice process system, you can talk about what he is doing and any ideas you might have that will help him.

By offering your experience, you are showing that you care about the success of others. That will win you points with your teammates. And by going outside your job responsibilities, you are showing your manager that you are a leader who looks beyond your job to help others.

Sam wasn't necessarily looking for someone to mentor. But one day the manager of a company call center found himself at the same lunch table as Sam in the company cafeteria. During the lunch conversation, the manager mentioned that he had a provider relations problem that he couldn't resolve. He casually asked Sam, a respected, senior-level manager, if he had any thoughts. Sam offered a few, off-the-top-of-his-head suggestions, then finished his turkey and cheese on whole wheat.

The next day, at lunch, the department head slid into the seat at the table across from Sam. It didn't take long for him to steer the conversation back to the provider relations issue. The lunch meetings went on for a week. Each day Sam helped the department head peel back another layer of the provider relations dilemma. With Sam's guidance, the department head fixed the problem and, as a bonus, saved the company $250,000 a year. Since the company had several call centers with the identical issue, that savings was multiplied many times over. The department head, and his mentor, had made a big impression on their bosses.

GOOD MENTORS STOP BAD CAREER DECISIONS

As a mentor, you should use your elevated position in the company to fly air cover for the person you are mentoring. So, if you think something is happening inside the company that will adversely affect him, don't hesitate to tell him and provide a few alternatives. How can you tip him off without betraying confidences? Just as Mary did. The person she was mentoring told Mary that he was frustrated and tired of waiting for the job he wanted to open up in his department. She reminded him that in a bad economy the company was not promoting people and that he should just be patient. He told her he was thinking about taking a job in another division. Mary knew that serious changes were in store for the division he was thinking about. All she said was, "You may not want to do that." Without another word from Mary, the employee got the message. He trusted that Mary was looking out for him and stayed put. A week later, the division he was considering was shut down.

53. Offer to Help New Employees

You don't have to be a mentor to help a colleague. All you really need to do is extend your hand to a new employee.

How will that save your job in bad times? By offering to help someone, you become a positive force within the company. And being seen in that light is one of the best ways to bulletproof your job. Being positive draws people to you. Because of your positive energy, other employees look to you for reassurance when things are bad. Your status allows you to rally your coworkers to finish a job on time, pitch in when a team member needs help, and speak for your coworkers if they have a grievance with management.

It doesn't matter to your colleagues that you are not the department's official leader. They follow your lead because your actions have earned you a fortune in trust and respect. Your clout comes from your positive personality, not the title after your name. If you were a professional athlete, you would be considered the "heart and soul" of your team, the person who provides the drive and emotion. And there is not a manager in his right mind who wants to rip the heart and soul out of his team.

A great way to build that influence is helping new employees feel at home. During times when jobs are hard to keep and even harder to find, people join a company for the paycheck. They may not know about the company or its role in the bigger world. Explaining why the company is successful, its goals, and how it intends to fulfill its aim, begins to bring them on board. In other words, teach the new employee about the business.

For new employees to feel a part of the business, they must understand how what they do fits into the overall picture. By connecting their job to a value, you increase the chances that they will become engaged, committed, and more focused on producing a quality product. Also, make it a point to introduce new employees to people in other parts of the organization as a way to lay the foundation for their growth and future success. Finally, as new employees receive assignments, be there to explain how each task relates to their job. You can also challenge them to use their job to find ways to save the company money. If, with your encouragement, they do develop a new idea that gets them positive feedback, you probably have helped establish some long-term employees. And it was all because you took the time to extend a hand.

The fact that you have taken a new employee under your wing isn't lost on your manager. She realizes the wonderful service you are performing. What service, you ask? Well, you are a one-person retention committee. Look, even when jobs are scarce, people still quit, or must be cut loose. In either case, that means your manager has to, once again, conduct a search, interview people, then hire and train them. Moreover, she has to do it without missing a beat on her other responsibilities, like keeping the department running smoothly. Moreover, that doesn't take into account the monetary cost incumbent in the process. By spending time guiding a new employee, you are saving your manager time and your company money, by reducing costly turnover. So, although your motives are pure—to ease someone into the mainstream of your

company—you will be repaid handsomely in the job-saving gratitude of your manager and the company.

PLAYER-COACH

Another way to protect your job is by becoming a
player-coach. A down economy is usually accompanied
by a thinning of the employee ranks. That means, of
course, more work for the people still employed. But it
also presents a great opportunity to become a player-
coach. In sports, a player-coach is someone who man-
ages the team while still playing in the field. That definition pretty much holds for business. As a player-coach,
you are still a working part of the project team or committee—rolling up your sleeves and getting involved in
the nitty-gritty—while assuming a leadership role. It's
going to mean more hours and responsibility. So, when
deciding to become a player-coach, choose the project
wisely.

54. Learn to Manage Conflict

If you can establish yourself as someone who helps people
resolve their differences, especially during difficult fiscal times
when your manager has his hands full, you can increase your
value significantly and save your job.

Managing conflict is a tremendously valuable skill set at any
time. But when the economy is slumping and managers need
people working together well, it is invaluable. Your conflict management sideline will probably, at first, be on an informal basis.
How it starts matters less than where it leads you.

When two people are at war, they usually don't see anything but their own position. Your job, then, is to begin the

conversation. Say you are in a meeting when a simmering feud between two of your colleagues erupts into an open war. That is your opportunity to get involved. Say something like, "I have an idea about how we might address this conflict." Ask to meet with each side alone. For you to be successful, you must remain, throughout the entire conflict management process, a neutral, uninterested third party. You must also possess a sterling reputation for being authentic and a nongossiper.

During the meeting, have each person clarify his or her position. Using that information, ask them next to suspend their points of view so that they can consider their adversary's position. For this technique to work, both parties must be truly interested in listening to the other person's viewpoint. They can prove their interest in resolving the conflict by asking probing questions to dig deeper into the issue. Then, request that each side articulate the merits of the other person's argument.

The next step is the trickiest. You must get the warring factions to emotionally detach from their respective side of the argument. If either one or both sides can't separate emotionally, the conflict could go unresolved. Bu if both sides agree to examine just the facts, you likely will discover that the clash is not about the people, but about an object.

The next step is to bring the two parties together and ask them to listen to and appreciate the other's view. Help the factions find the critical points where they really disagree and then ask them to brainstorm together to find a compromise solution. The idea is to reach a win/win for both sides.

You can use the same method for healing chronic differences between two departments. The more conflicts you help resolve, the more your manager will recognize your value and view you as having a special, essential talent.

Part III

Keep Your Job by
Helping the Company

As an employee, it is sometimes hard to sympathize with how the owner is operating the company. But when the economy has flamed out, the only way for the company to survive is for employees to begin thinking and acting like owners.

Before you can begin thinking like an owner, you first must decide whether or not you want to be part of the rescue effort. If you choose to stay and help, you must understand and accept that you may be agreeing to deferring, or even forgoing, a salary raise or annual bonus, while accepting a lot more work and responsibility. Also, you must buy into, and practice, the company's core values. It means not just doing your job but embracing it, and recognizing that your success is intrinsically connected to the company's success.

Acting like an owner requires you to see and understand the business from different viewpoints—worker, manager, owner—all at once. Acting like an owner means being aware of how your workers feel and why, the pressure and strain experienced by the managers, and the staggering responsibility the owner has for everyone. When you act like an owner, you have to make hard decisions that are not based on what is best for you but what is best for everyone who works for you.

As an employee learning to act like an owner, your first and foremost task is to do your job well. After that, it is to help your colleagues and the company succeed together.

The most direct way to help your company through enigmatic economic times is root out waste to save money. You can bet your paycheck that your company's bean counters are not just scrutinizing every expense; they're also telling the appropriate people who is, and who isn't, belt tightening. So why draw negative attention to yourself? Before you pull out your company credit card, stop and think about whether what you are purchasing is really necessary. And instead of taking the scenic route the next time you call on your client, save some gasoline costs by using a more direct path.

All those dollars you save the company will eventually add up. But even more importantly, your manager will notice. Why? Because most employees think that the only way to contribute to the company's bottom line is by bringing money in. By cutting your costs, you are showing your manager that you understand that saving money is just as important to the company as money earned.

So, in your effort to save the company money and, in turn, your job, think little and big. Your job, especially when business is bad, is to scour your department and company for ways to lower costs. Every idea you come up with may not work. But the fact that you are trying to cut costs may just impress your manager enough to help save your job.

In the end why you decide to stick around—at least you still have a job—is nobody's business. The only thing that counts is that you are willing to roll up your sleeves and grab an oar and pull in unison with everyone else. It may not seem like much, but your manager will view you not only as a positive, consummate team player and leader, but as a person whose personal values include a trait that is rare in today's business world: loyalty. If the company survives—and with people like you, why wouldn't it?—that can take your career a long way.

55. Take the Tough Job

You can earn management's respect and ensure your job security by stepping up and offering to tackle the toughest problem facing your manager. And what better time to demonstrate traits like initiative, courage, and leadership than when you are trying to keep your job?

But before you sign on, you will want to talk through the assignment with your manager to set up job parameters and define the meaning of success. Even if you casually discussed taking on the task, review again the nature of the problem, its complexity, and your strategy for attacking the challenge. Make sure you are clear about what your manager wants. Is this an all-or-nothing situation? Do you have to resolve the entire issue, not just a piece of it? Just as important, you want your manager to understand that, while you are fully committed to finding an answer to the vexing problem, you cannot guarantee that you can fix it.

After you share your ideas about how to retire the lingering issue, ask your manager if he agrees with your plan, and is on board and committed to your blueprint. You want to lock down your manager's total backing because, somewhere along the line, you are going to need him readily available for his advice, support, resources, and, if necessary, the time to work directly with you. You also want your manager's buy-in because:

✔ This is a high-profile project. If things go badly, you don't want to be the scapegoat.
✔ If your manager signs on, you are more likely to get all the resources you need to succeed.

Getting your manager's buy-in is important, but not critical. Look, you really aren't taking a great risk by volunteering for the "tough job." It's the "tough job" for a reason. People have been trying to slay this beast for a while. Sure, you may be shining a flashlight into a black hole, but the worst that is going to happen is you join the ranks of those who tried and failed. Hey, as the saying goes, some days you eat the bear, and some days the bear eats you.

The good news about taking on the tough job is the upside potential. It is tremendous. If you do resolve the problem, you become not just the fair-haired boy or girl, but you have a job with the company until it sells the furniture and locks the doors. So get to work dissecting and laying out whatever facts you have like pieces of a puzzle to see if anything fits together. Just sorting out and separating the issues into distinct groupings may put you head and shoulders above everyone else who has ever gotten into the ring. Ask for as much help as you can get, so that you have other people working on side issues while you stay focused on the overall problem.

If you realize that your best plan to solve the enigma has failed, it may be time to go to plan B—attacking one aspect of the multilayered problem. Check back with your manager for his approval on your course of action. If you get the green light, ask him what section of the puzzle is causing him the greatest concern, or he would most like resolved. Then focus on unraveling that tangle.

Be aware that there are pitfalls to taking a piecemeal approach. Sometimes the answers to individual parts of a larger problem do not fit well with an overall solution. If you do nothing else, try your best to move the ball forward as much as possible.

56. Drum Up Business

When a business is in trouble, every employee becomes a salesperson. From the mail room to the board room, everyone has to pitch in to find new revenue streams. Your job description, in some cases, will dictate what you can do to drum up business. But aside from the obvious reason of keeping the company solvent, you want to be part of the effort to round up new business, to show management that you are willing to go beyond your normal responsibilities to help. Your company-first attitude will definitely contribute to your job security.

If you work in sales, remember the axiom that says a successful salesperson is constantly growing his or her network. So dig up and develop fresh leads by attending conferences or other professional meetings. But be choosy. You want to talk to people in your business concentration. So, if your company is in the health-care industry and you specialize in MRI equipment sales, focus your time. Talk to people associated with diagnostic medicine. It is one thing to get contacts in health care. But it is far better to develop contacts in your specific area. The more prospects you have, the better the chance of converting one into a client. Plus, those people can give you more new names, and so on and so on.

When you meet with potential clients, be uber-prepared. It's a given that you know your product or service inside out. But if you want to exponentially increase your chances of nabbing the contract, demonstrate to a prospective client that you understand the nuts and bolts of her business, as well as the basics of her clients. As you expand your network, call your regular clients and tell them what you are doing. Don't be shy. Come right out and ask for a referral. Really, if your customer likes you, why wouldn't he be willing to match you with someone who can use your product or service? Also, remember that the easiest new sale is an old sale. The money from a repeat customer counts toward your company's bottom line as much as the money from a new one. Customers like doing business with people they trust. So work at creating a bond with your clients by being honest and fair, and by providing products and services that solve their problems. Think of your clients as your business partners and give them the kind of service you would want and expect.

Part of drumming up business is investing time with your clients. So call them just to chat. Stop in if you are in the area. Ask how things are going, and if there is anything you can do for them. Send birthday, holiday, and special occasion cards. You want to keep your name and face fresh in your client's mind so that when an opportunity arises, she immediately thinks of you.

57. Go Easy on Expenses

If you treat your expense budget like it is your own checking account, you will greatly enhance the chances of keeping your job.

The corporate expense account is probably the most abused budget line in American business. And don't think your manager isn't paying attention to yours, especially if it changes when she is with you. Let's say you and your boss take a client to lunch. When the bill comes, you put it on your expense account and add a fifteen percent tip. That's a fair amount. But your manager, who goes over every expense account you submit, knows that when she isn't there, you always tip twenty percent. Now you have tripped your manager's expense-account padding alarm, which leads her to scrutinize every bill you submit. And sure enough, your manager begins to notice a pattern emerging.

When your manager is along, you are a conservative diner, ordering a chicken entrée, a glass of house wine, and no dessert. But when your manager isn't there, you are Mr. Big Spender gourmet, cutting into a prime filet, an expensive bottle of wine, and the dessert sampler. Clearly, you are the expense-account equivalent of Dr. Jekyll and Mr. Hyde. Obviously, when the boss isn't looking over your tab, you don't give a hoot about conserving company money.

Eating well on the company may seem like a little thing, to you. But when a company is struggling to stay afloat, every dollar counts. Perhaps more to the point, the company, and specifically your manager, expects you to trim your expenses where possible. The fact that you only do so when being watched, reveals a cynical, anti-company attitude. That reflects badly on your manager, which can lead to resentment.

Is it enough resentment to throw you overboard? Probably not, especially if you are a big revenue producer. Even if you're not a money person, a good manager isn't likely to can you because you bought a $50 bottle of wine instead of a $20 bottle. But don't fool yourself. Your free spending on your expense account has raised your profile on the radar screen. The question for you is, does it pay to have your boss silently fuming over a bottle of wine and steak dinner at a time when your job could be on the line?

So what should you do? Keep in mind that those little, day-to-day decisions you make not only add up, but are being watched. So make fiscally prudent choices. Nobody says you can't take a client to lunch to seal a deal. Nor would anyone expect you to ask a client to order a less expensive meal. But you can downsize the price of your meal. And you can also scale back the price of your wine selection. Your major contribution to the company may be the revenue you generate. But don't limit it to that. You can also kick in by finding ways to save money for the company. Your manager will quickly forget your largess at the company's expense if you reduce your expense account bills and introduce some cost-cutting ideas.

BIG SPENDERS LOSE AN EMPLOYEE

After the final meeting interview where he was offered the job, Chris agreed to have a celebratory drink with his new colleagues. His new coworkers wined and dined Chris, including draining several bottles of wine at $150 a bottle. Chris was taken aback by the free spending. When the bill came, Chris was stunned by the amount his colleagues-to-be had spent. He offered to throw in some cash to defray the cost but was told not to worry because the company could afford to pay for it. Later that night, at home, Chris thought that if people at the company were so nonchalant about running up their expense accounts, how committed were they to the business succeeding? The next morning, Chris called and turned down the job offer.

Just because you're not in sales doesn't mean you can't create business. For instance, you can write a white paper on a topic of interest to your client. Or perhaps you can generate a brochure on what your department has to offer and send it to other groups in the organization. If you work in the mail room, take a look at how much the company is spending on parcels and overnight deliveries. Then make a few calls to see if you can get a better price. The company's bottom line doesn't discriminate between money saved and new revenue coming in.

Finally, look around the company to see if any part of the business is being underutilized. For instance, if your company runs a call center that has excess capacity, why not suggest contracting with smaller businesses to do their telephone work? Your company has the knowledge, the equipment, and the time. And when business is down, it can use new-found money.

58. Find Ways to Save Money

Along with curbing charges on your expense account, there are several other ways to help your company save money. And remember, every dollar you conserve accrues interest in the very important save-your-job account.

While anyone in any department can find ways to cut costs, rooting out waste becomes urgent if your department or team is not part of the company's core business. The more distant your group is from the company's reason for being, the more likely it will be eliminated or sharply downsized when management begins looking for ways to save. The more your department can tighten its own belt, the better its chances of surviving. Managers and executives are unlikely to close a department that is in the black.

When it comes to saving money, look, well, everywhere. Nothing should be sacred. You can find extra pennies to millions of dollars by simply strolling through the business and observing how it functions. For instance, somewhere along your walk, you will probably see someone sitting idly at her desk. Your first impulse is to think that firing the lazy slacker would be a fast way to save the company money. Not so fast there, you Montgomery Burns wannabe. Employees who look like they are loafing are, many times, the victims of an out-of-sync business process. They can't do their job until someone else completes another job. So, the savings aren't in slashing your coworker's job. They lie in finding a way to make the process more streamlined and efficient.

Your job, then, is to break down the breakdown. Figure out if it would help to have people who depend on each other's work sit closer together so that they can communicate better? Perhaps the issue is in a different part of the process. For instance, if you only use five lines of a twenty-five line form, can you redo the form to make it quicker? Or maybe people are still performing unnecessary processes left over from one of the organization's earlier incarnations. Find the answer and reap the savings.

Where else should you look? You may be able to save money in the department's contractual agreements. Go over each one with a fine-toothed comb. Identify areas that you want to renegotiate, and then contact the vendor. Most vendors and suppliers are surprisingly open to renegotiating the current agreement if they think it could be the difference between winning or losing a future contract.

Now, do the same thing in the human resources department. Health benefits chew up a huge portion of a company's income. So ask the HR manager to discuss ways to lower premium rates with the company's health-care provider. The provider may suggest a different health-care package that will lower rates and save the company money, even if it is just for the short term.

If your company has an advertising budget, approach the ad agency with a similar pitch. Also, study the company's marketing budget to see if you can reduce or eliminate the marketing brochures. Stop printing the company newsletter, to save on paper, ink, and transportation costs. Instead, make the newsletter available online.

As for conventions, measure the amount of business the company receives from each event, and cut out the least financially fruitful. Business travel, in general, should be curtailed. Video conferencing is the next best thing to being there, and a lot cheaper. If the trip is necessary, book the lowest fares and accommodations. If the company has frequent airline or train miles, don't forget to use them.

In a recession, almost every company is going to reduce its staff. The key to keeping your job is standing out in the crowd, and doing a great job, frankly, isn't enough. A lot of people do good work. You have to make a compelling argument for yourself. One way to separate yourself from the herd is by showing your manager that you know how to find ways to save the company money.

59. Develop an Anti-Gossip Plan

Gossip can be a company's downfall because it can polarize groups of employees and erode the fabric of a department or team. To help your manager keep the department working together as a unit, offer to establish an office anti-gossip plan. By creating a plan to defuse the insidious and often hurtful problem that will eventually cripple your team or department, you will earn your manager's gratitude. And there's no better way to save your job than to have your manager's gratitude.

Human beings love gossip. The strange need to know the secrets and problems of celebrities is the engine that sells millions of magazines like *People* and *US Weekly* every week. In that context, gossip is fairly harmless. But in an office setting, gossip is nothing less than poison. It ruins productivity, makes coworkers wary of each other, and undermines teamwork, especially during a downturn in business activity.

Becoming part of the office gossip grapevine can happen innocently enough. Gossip surrounds you in an office setting. Gossip is really about controlling information and deciding who can and cannot have it. It works like this: John tells you a secret. Now you know something that no one else but you and John know. That means you have power. But the only way to prove you have power is to share the secret, which is where the Catch-22 comes in. To demonstrate your power, you must reveal the secret. But the irony is, when you tell the secret, you aren't flexing your power. Rather, you are telling your coworkers that you are an untrustworthy gossipmonger. And once you do that, do you really think anyone in the office will trust you?

So, rather than get sucked into the gossip cycle, be proactive and try to stop gossiping before it infects your department like a virus, causing decreased productivity and unending sniping. Get your manager to let you develop an anti-gossip policy and call a department meeting. After you make it clear that you have the full support of your manager, explain to everyone the dangers inherent in gossip. Then encourage people to talk about the ways gossip has led to misunderstandings or hurt their careers in the past. Lay out ground rules for the air-clearing session, like not allowing names to be used. Then ask everyone to vow to politely accept, with a positive attitude, reminders about the new policy if they are caught gossiping.

Form an anti-gossip committee from among your peers. If there are known gossips in the group, make a point of asking them to join the committee. Charge the committee with developing an anti-gossip program along with ways to police the policy. For instance, the committee may hang anti-gossip posters around the office to remind people about the policy. It may also send interoffice e-mail reminding people not to spread rumors.

To put some bite behind the anti-gossip program's bark, ask your manager to include the issue as an item on each person's job performance evaluation. If you have a serious gossiping problem, ask your manager to consider reducing raises or bonuses for repeat offenders.

On the other edge of the anti-gossip sword, create a peace plan. The idea of the peace plan is to help smooth over relationships damaged by gossip. Ask your coworkers not to act deceitful or misrepresent what other people say for personal gain. The peace plan can also be used as an intervention tool to defuse contentious situations. The last thing a business already stressed by a faltering market needs is internal strife.

Combined, the anti-gossip program and peace plan can reduce office tension and create a harmonious atmosphere. And as is already known, a happy office is a productive office.

60. Develop a Disaster Plan

If your organization doesn't have a disaster plan, offer to develop one. Creating a disaster plan probably won't save your job on its own. But it will show your manager that, should a disaster strike, you have the best interest of your department and the company at heart. She will also recognize that you are a take-contol type of person who understands that having a plan in place will help the organization survive the crisis.

Disasters can be natural or man-made. Most companies have insurance protection against natural disasters like earthquakes,

134 HOW TO KEEP YOUR JOB . . .

floods, tornados, hurricanes, blizzards, ice storms, and fire. Man-made calamities can range from computer crashes or viruses, someone hacking into the company's computer, the sudden death of an executive, or office violence. Insurance is available to protect against financial loss or the breakdown of vital equipment.

But when a disaster befalls your office it usually hits suddenly and with devastating effects. With no disaster plan in place, people are left confused and unsure about what to do. For example, today's offices are bristling with sensitive, high-tech equipment that can crash, be hacked, or become infected with a virus. Your office needs a plan that addresses each event. Can you continue working, and if so, how? Most companies back up their computers every night. But what if it happens during work hours? To make sure her company isn't paralyzed, one office manager assigns one billing person to work from home each day. That way if there is a system failure, the offsite employee can continue processing bills.

So how do you develop a disaster plan? Once your manager agrees, convene a group of colleagues and begin discussing different types of disasters. Prod people to think about the unthinkable—a terrorist attack, office violence, or the on-the-job death of an employee, manager, or executive. Some people may balk because the topics are uncomfortable. But keep pushing. It is necessary to consider extreme disasters as a way to unveil the organization's vulnerabilities and risks, which you need to know in order to assess what action to take. But also, by conjuring up and talking about what to do during a nightmare scenario, you have a better chance of not freezing and being unable to function. Break the process into sections. For instance, for technology and equipment, ask and answer questions like:

✔ What should employees do if there is a power, telephone, or computer crash?
✔ Who should be called if there is a system failure?

✔ Who is responsible for efforts to recover lost data?
✔ How is recovery done?
✔ Who will pay for overtime?
✔ Who is responsible for routine maintenance of computers and equipment?
✔ How do you inform employees in the field about the problem?
✔ If applicable, how do you let your customers know?

The disaster plan should address what to do in case of a flood or fire, and include scheduling regular onsite inspections, an employee evacuation plan with a designated meeting place, and a recovery plan.

Create a specific disaster directive for dealing with bomb threats, a terrorist attack, or other office violence, including the phone numbers of the appropriate authorities to contact. If your office has an automatic defibrillator for heart attacks, make sure employees are trained in its use.

The committee should then create a brochure with the written protocols for all employees to follow.

61. Create an Orientation Schedule

Even when companies are contracting, new people are still brought on. So, if you hear about an addition, volunteer to do the new employee's orientation. You will be removing a chore from your manager's to-do list, while presenting yourself as a company-oriented, team player.

Approach your manager and say something like, "I understand we have a new employee joining us. I know how busy you are, so I'd like to help out by being responsible for their orientation." Ask the manager how long the orientation should last and what he would like you to cover during that time. Then, if you think something was left out, suggest it or any other ideas you might have.

Once the details are worked out, immediately send off a letter introducing yourself and welcoming the incoming employee. Include your e-mail address, phone number, and extension, and let the new employee know that she should feel free to contact you with any questions before her first day of work.

If your company doesn't have an orientation folder, create one by pulling together important pieces of pertinent information. The folder should contain:

✔ A company organization chart.
✔ An office directory.
✔ The department's emergency plan.
✔ Important outside phone numbers.
✔ The department's downtime plan.

Have an orientation schedule ready the day the new person arrives. It should include visits to important office locations as well as common areas, such as the lunchroom, bathrooms, and employee lounge. Also carve out time for the employee to spend with the information technology people so the employee can receive a password and whatever technical training is necessary to familiarize her with the company's computer system.

If professional training is needed, make sure the instructor knows what job the new employee will be performing and the skill sets necessary.

On the social side, choose a staff member to introduce the new person to other members of the organization. Make sure the staff member has some of the incoming employee's background information—for example, the names of her spouse and children, and where she lives—to make her feel comfortable and help keep a conversation going.

As part of the orientation, build in time to meet with the employee to review her progress, go over goals, and talk about the next phase. Also ask for feedback from the employee about her experience so far. Make time to discuss the office culture, including dress code, personal appearance, what is and isn't considered acceptable behavior, and what office meetings and functions she will be expected to attend.

When the orientation concludes, do one last review and assure the new hire that you are still available to answer questions and provide guidance. In essence, you are making the latest staff addition part of your network, and perhaps you may become their mentor. Either way, it's good for both of you.

Of course, your manager will expect a report. If you really want to impress him and showcase your management skills, file your report with an orientation evaluation form rating the new employee's orientation experience in both objective and subjective ways. Who knows, you may become your department's orientation expert.

62. Clear the Air

The world is standing on the threshold of a green revolution. Cleaning up the environment and saving the earth from global warming are high on the agendas of every government across the planet. Yet, inside some office buildings, the air is terribly polluted by fumes from chemical cleaners, printing and copying machines, and biological contaminants, as well as particles from drywall and even furniture and carpeting.

The office's air quality is certainly not going to be at the top of your manager's list of issues to address, especially when the business is circling the drain. So make it your business to clear the air. It will help you keep your job by demonstrating to your manager and others your commitment to the physical health and well-being of your coworkers and, in turn, the financial fortunes of the company.

Poor indoor air quality greatly increases the risk of spreading disease and illness throughout the company. Several studies conducted over the years by the United States Environmental Protection Agency (EPA) have shown that indoor air quality is a serious health threat. And if employees are forced to take more sick time, it will eventually translate into a drop in production for the company and lost revenue.

While most buildings don't have major air pollution issues, it doesn't take much to foul the air inside an office. A malfunction in the building's ventilation system, some nearby construction, or a buildup of mold from leaks can quickly foul the air inside the best buildings. But "sick" buildings share some traits in common:

✔ There is a low intake of outdoor air.
✔ The structure is sealed with centralized air and heating.
✔ There have been maintenance problems with the heating and air conditioning.
✔ A large portion of the workforce uses computer equipment.
✔ There are large areas of carpeting and upholstered furniture.

By being aware of how people act and feel in your office, the EPA says, most indoor air problems can be easily prevented or corrected. All it takes is getting people to work together and using a little common sense. To help, you could ask coworkers to do the following:

✔ Do not block air vents.
✔ Clean up water spills.
✔ Add office plants.

✔ Report leaks right away.
✔ Dispose of garbage.
✔ Store food properly.

When you assume responsibility for keeping your office's air safe and clean, you can develop a set of guidelines for management and your coworkers to follow. If your company doesn't own the building, you will want to establish a good working relationship with the building management to ensure the greatest amount of cooperation. Inside your office, make sure air supply vents are not blocked by furniture or equipment. Be particularly aware that computers produce enough heat to trigger the air conditioning, even when it isn't needed. That could result in employees' feeling cold or uncomfortable, which in turn can lead to a slip in their work production.

If your office is like most, you probably have an array of copiers, fax machines, and printing machines, which release pollutants and odors. Make sure these items are all placed in an area with adequate ventilation. When purchasing new furniture or equipment, ask the vendor to provide information, when possible, about chemical fumes that items may release. You are most interested in chemicals associated with respiratory hazards.

Most companies have strict no-smoking policies. If your company does not, immediately establish your department as a smoke-free zone. Since most people know the health risks to both smokers and nonsmokers exposed to secondhand smoke, you should have no problem getting it approved. Once you have a policy and program in place, everyone in your office will breathe easier. And your manager will have you to thank for her employees taking fewer sick days and exceeding production quotas.

63. Create an Alumni Directory

Did you ever wonder what happened to Marlene after she left the company? Or what Bill, the guy from the IT department who moved away, is up to these days? If you really want to find out, and in the process throw another log on the save-your-job bonfire, volunteer to create an online alumni directory.

Alumni directories are an easy, inexpensive, and smart way for your company to keep track of its former employees. Colleges and universities have long recognized the value of alumni directories, beginning eons ago with newsletters. Today, most institutions of higher learning have an online alumni network and e-mail centers. Outside of higher education, online sites for professionals, like LinkedIn, employ the same strategy. The difference is that your site would focus solely on your company's former workers. But why would your company want to know what its *ex*-employees are up to? Because you just never know how you can utilize them.

There was a time when, if you left a job, you were dead to that company. Not anymore. Companies today are not as paternalistic toward employees. A company is less likely to view one of its employees' leaving as a betrayal. Business executives recognize that the nature of work has changed. People are more mobile and leave for any number of reasons. So there is no reason to feel slighted or offended by an employee's switching jobs. If the separation was amicable, there is absolutely no reason not to stay in touch with your former coworkers. If you keep in contact, the former employee can be an ambassador, or more, for your company.

For many companies, the main incentive to stay in touch is the opportunity to lure someone back into the fold. Rehiring a former employee costs much less than bringing on a fresh hire. Also, he or she is a known quantity. In a down business cycle, however, rehiring isn't going to be of interest to your company. So, tell your manager that there are other ways to extract value from former employees. For starters, they may become your company's newest client. Or they may turn out to be a great referral. Of course, one of your former workers may have gone on to become a VIP in the industry.

Unless you know your way around a computer, you may need help from someone in the IT department to set up a website, with a link to the company's main page. The heart of the site would be the alumni directory, where former colleagues who have moved on to other positions can locate and contact each other. Other items the site could include are an e-mail service, company news with targeted information or stories, marketing initiatives, an events calendar for alumni luncheons or parties, and general announcements. You might even consider an alumnus-of-the-month section.

The alumni directory site is also a great way to manage alumni perception of your company by bringing ex-employees up-to-date on what is happening at your company. And who knows, a former employee or two from time to time may offer a fresh perspective about a project he or she sees on the site. In fact, having an alumni directory may prove so beneficial to the company that it will be clear to everyone involved that your job should be saved.

64. Become the Agent of Change

As your organization moves through change, you can help guide it by cooperating with your manager and being a steadying influence on your department. Your manager will appreciate your positive attitude and willingness to become actively involved in the change process. Beside winning her gratitude, you will impress your manager in a way that will help secure your job.

People resist change for any number of reasons. In some cases, people don't understand intellectually why the company needs, or has decided, to alter the course of business, or why it has chosen a specific direction. Without more information concerning why the company made the choices it did, those people will remain in opposition to change.

Another group of employees will resist change because they are unsure of what change means for them and their job security. The more their fear and anxiety rise, the more these employees will dig in, developing a siege mentality that will make them fight change to the end.

Still another group of employees are simply opposed to or afraid of the demands that change will make on them. They are concerned that change will require them to modify their routine and force them to do things differently. These employees may also be worried that they will not measure up in the new environment. They may harbor doubts as to whether or not they are capable of mastering new skills, techniques, or behaviors. They simply may not want to take on any new responsibilities demanded by change.

You can help your coworkers, and by extension your manager, by providing a rationale and information about the company's direction. You may well have to hold some hands to help people through the change, but your calm demeanor will begin to alleviate some of the concerns within your group or department. Be an example for people by modeling the behavior that management wants from your colleagues. Show people that you support the changes by being openly cooperative with your manager. Don't go over the top. Your actions must be tactful and authentic. You do not want your coworkers to perceive you as acting differently.

You can help people in your department work through change by being a resource for your colleagues. Pull together as a department. Encourage everyone to pitch in so that you can do more with less. Organize informal meetings where you can talk about ways to make the department more efficient, streamline processes, or change the way work gets done. Find ways to bring people together. Build coalitions inside and outside the department. And be ready to remove roadblocks to progress when they arise.

Another way you can help your manager is by monitoring the mood of the organization. When your company is undergoing change, your manager is sure to be overwhelmed with work. He won't have the time or the energy to keep his finger firmly on the department's pulse. Again, you can help make the manager's job easier, while showing your colleagues that you support change. If you sense a downswing in the group's mood, or if you notice the program isn't working, let your manager know. Likewise, if he is about to implement a decision that you think will have the opposite of the desired effect, tactfully bring it up.

You can also help out by keeping everyone informed about important issues or topics inside your company or industry by reading newsletters, websites, and blogs. And just to make sure you cover all the angles, check in occasionally to see what your competition is doing.

65. Control Your Anxiety

The last thing a manager needs when business is bad are anxiety-ridden employees. But that is precisely what he has. People respond to pending changes at work in many different ways, but most commonly employees are anxious. Every time the boss walks by, he could be coming to say those fateful words, "Sorry Tina, but we're going to have to let you go."

It should come as no surprise, then, that anxious employees are more apt to resist workplace change than embrace it.

Ironically, by resisting, you are actually increasing your risk of being among the first to go from employed to unemployed. With fear of sounding like a 1950s sci-fi alien invasion movie, when it comes to change, "It is futile to resist."

Being awash in anxiety is part of an emotional cycle almost every employee goes through when change is underway at work. The key to keeping your job, of course, is to control your anxiety so you don't become a huge burden to your manager, and to then move through the minefield of emotions as quickly as possible.

For someone locked in place by anxiety, that is easier said than done. But you can do it. Actually, you must do it, and your manager can help. Most managers are trained or can get help for employees frozen by anxiety. Because your manager understands the urgency of having everyone pulling together to make the coming change smooth and successful, she will try different ways to motivate you, while helping you shake off your anxiety and resistance to change. Will she hold your hand and tell you everything is going to be all right? Probably not. But that verbal poke you feel every so often is your manager's way of saying, "Wake up. You can't continue to sit there and be blind to the fact that the company needs to change and is moving along without you."

If you want to keep your job, take your manager's advice—stop being anxious and start facing reality. You must get yourself unstuck before it is too late. The faster you can reach the low point of the anxiety/depression cycle and bounce back up, the better your chance of surviving change. People who prefer to believe that all will be well if they just ignore the change occurring around them, or otherwise bury their heads, have an almost zero chance of staying employed. Walking around mumbling about how unfair the company is, or cursing your lot in the world, is only earning you a bad reputation, destroying your brand, and sinking your career.

Change is an almost unstoppable force. You must jar yourself out of the deer-frozen-in-the-headlights attitude and get moving in the right direction. So, as quickly as possible, acknowledge that you are anxious and that is why you are resisting change. Then, admit that you cannot stop change and that you must come to terms with your situation immediately.

A good way to tamp down any lingering feelings of anxiety is by tuning into another basic emotion—survival. That's right, be honest with yourself and lay out all the cards on the table. If you think you are anxious now, just think about how high the anxiety level will be cranked up when you're unemployed. Now, consider the possibilities that change offers—new opportunities, new challenges, job promotions. Change just might not be so bad, after all.

If you don't take control of your career, you risk becoming stuck in place like a statue. Losing your job won't be so much a matter of change as it is a self-fulfilling prophecy. Self-empowerment separates the people who will keep their jobs from those who are left behind by change.

66. Be Positive about Change

Change may be what people want from politicians. But uttering the word *change* in the workplace is like yelling fire in a movie theater. Nobody likes it and will do everything in their power to avoid it. The word unleashes immediate panic among workers.

And why not? Change is almost always guaranteed to lift you from your comfort zone and deposit you into the unknown. At work, it may mean the loss of power, title, office, and even a job.

Nevertheless, change is the hallmark of employment in the twenty-first century. The rules governing how companies grow, thrive, and remain successful are constantly being rewritten. So common is news of the demise of an industry leader that people hardly raise an eyebrow. Business has become a bare-knuckled brawl for survival. Doors are closing and companies are merging. Survival means businesses must be flexible, creative, and innovative. In short, it means that business and its employees will be under constant pressure to change.

The best way to keep your job in a change environment is to become adaptable. Recognize that change is inevitable and there is usually nothing you can do to stop it. What you can do is control your attitude. If you choose to fight change, it will plow you off to the side of the road like yesterday's snow. Adopt a positive attitude, and change holds the prospect of wonderful, new opportunities.

Almost every employee facing change is worried about what he or she will lose or be forced to give up because of it. In particular, employees are concerned about the loss of personal relationships with colleagues and their manager. They want to know if the change will affect the evaluation system and work conditions, and to whom they will report.

As an employee who wants to keep your job, you must adopt a positive attitude and work to ensure a smooth transition. Feelings of insecurity and even fear are perfectly normal during change. Talk to your manager and anyone in senior management willing to give you the time about why change is necessary and how it will ultimately help the company. Evaluate what you are told. Be realistic and try to understand the reasons you have been given. Also, recognize that change can offer a new perspective and introduce new ideas that can re-energize the company. Then, figure out where you fit in this new business world.

If employees look to you during upheaval, be careful about what you say and how you say it. Any angst in your voice will be like spraying gasoline on a fire. Listen to what your colleagues are saying, and try to help them work through their issues. The natural reaction to loss is resistance. Explain that resisting change will only make the experience harder. But even more important, be honest. Tell them that, more than the change itself, their resistance will put their job in jeopardy.

67. Get Inside Change

Being positive about change is something you absolutely must do if you don't want to lose your job immediately. But if you want a real shot at keeping your job, become part of the change machinery. Getting plugged in to the change plan that affects your department will help you keep your job by funneling insider information to you. Plus, because you are now part of the change team, management will view you in a positive light.

There are several ways that you can step up and actively help your manager and the company manage the transition from point A to point B. Your manager will almost surely need help monitoring plans and milestones. But maintaining communication with employees will probably be her highest priority. A smooth transformation demands that employees be kept apprised of what is happening.

But even managers who have been through the change cycle before and recognize the angst it can cause among employees, need help staying in the loop. You can become that liaison between your coworkers and management.

Before you agree to be the informal liaison, be clear with your manager that you aren't interested in betraying coworkers' confidences, like tipping off the boss that Brian is looking for another job. First of all, that is confidential information. Secondly, if you reveal that kind of information, even if your manager directly asks for it, she may no longer trust you. Where you will have to make a judgment call is if your manager tells you that she really wants to keep Brian and you know that Brian is interviewing for other jobs.

The best way to help your manager and colleagues is by giving organization temperature readings. Use yourself as an example to explain the emotions people are feeling and why they may be reacting in a particular way. Once you have your manager's ear, talk about the concerns that the unspooling change has unleashed. Again, voice your personal feelings to verify and validate what other people are experiencing. You can also offer ideas and suggestions about how your manager can acknowledge employee anxiety. If people would like to see or hear something specific from your manager, tell her. For instance, if employees would like more direct face time, maybe you can set up a weekly lunch gathering. You can also create an issues agenda that your manager can use to talk to people about during the day. You can also remind your manager to acknowledge the good things happening in the office, and the small successes.

The more you pitch in and identify problems and issues for your manager, the better life will be for everyone in the department. The most important thing is to keep the dialogue flowing between the boss and employees. The last thing employees, you, your manager, and the company want is silence. A management information blackout makes people anxious and causes productivity to fall. For change to proceed smoothly, people need to hear and be heard.

68. Keep Tabs on Management's Direction

Keeping your job requires more effort from you beyond proving your value to the company. It also means that you invest the time to research and understand where the company is heading and why. Possessing that information not only keeps you abreast of management's current philosophy but allows you to separate the wheat from the chaff when it comes to rumors. And, on the off chance your boss asks, you can enhance your status by demonstrating a deeper understanding of the business.

Tracking your company's moves shouldn't be difficult if it is publicly held. To gain real insight into why the company operates the way it does, you may want to read about the company's history and its founders. More often than not, there is still a trace of the founder's influence in the present operation of the company. If you know where a company comes from, you have a better shot at understanding where it is going.

Search on Google for the names of the executives running the company to learn about their backgrounds. Talk to older colleagues who have spent their entire careers with the company. And don't forget the receptionist and janitor. You would be surprised how many closeted skeletons they know about.

For financial information, study the annual report and quarterly shareholder statements. Along with finances, the reports will pinpoint the company's strategic direction, its goals, and its performance against those goals. Both are public records and easily obtained. Also check out news sources like *The Wall Street Journal*, financial newspapers and magazines, as well as association and industry newsletters. Check out your company's main competition to see if it has altered its course in any way.

Of course, there is the company's website and online financial and industry websites. While surfing the Internet, don't forget to read industry-related blogs. And to make sure you cover both sides of the street, search on Google for your company's name to see if there are any negative websites and, if so, what is being said. Hey, keeping your job is about knowing the good and the bad.

Next, ask for a meeting with your manager. Be a good sport; let him know that you want to talk about the company's direction, what has changed, and what are the strategic priorities. Chances are he will have to make a few phone calls and read a couple of reports to prepare for your meeting. If your manager asks why you are interested, say that you are invested in the company and want to understand how management makes decisions.

If your manager is unwilling—which he should never be— or unable to brief you on the topics, ask him to refer you to someone from the CFO's office. Depending on the size of the company, there are usually people responsible for tracking the company's actual return against its stated goals.

When business is off, managers will frequently meet more often with employees. If your manager doesn't schedule those meetings, don't hesitate to request that he does. You will be doing him a favor, because when people sense that business is bad but are not given any information from management, they become anxious, pessimistic, and resistant to change.

During meetings with your manager, listen for what is said about a change in priorities or the goals for your department, and where the company wants to reduce spending. Where things have changed, ask your manager to explain why, and what the implications are for your group. Say something like, "If management is asking for a fifteen percent reduction in our spending, what does it translate to for our group, and how does it compare with what other departments have been asked to do?"

Ultimately you want to understand how changes in your department's priorities and goals line up with the direction the company is moving. You may discover that the company has less interest in your department's work. And that is precisely the kind of information you need if you want to save your job.

69. When the Company Does Well, You Succeed

It often takes a crisis threatening the existence of a company to make some employees understand just how much their success is intrinsically tied to the business's success. A dramatic downturn in the economy, accompanied by the specter of lost jobs, is just that kind of dire circumstance.

When your company is in trouble, you should immediately get involved and help. Choosing to stand on the sideline during an emergency will only make you an easy target if layoffs hit. So, lay aside any petty differences you may have with your manager or the company, and cast yourself in the role of a team player who wants a part in helping the business survive. While this isn't a time for self-promotion, pitching in will win you kudos from a management team desperate for all the help it can get. Along with earning positive reviews from the people that count, you have a front-row seat to the measures being taken to steady the listing company.

But your insider position automatically comes with a built-in responsibility. You will be expected to act as an emissary or spokesperson for the company to the people in your department or organization. Your job will be to fill everyone in on the details of the survival plan. You should tell your coworkers as much as you can, without disclosing privileged information. And don't guess or speculate about anything. If someone asks you a question that you can't answer—either because you don't know or aren't permitted—just say so.

Joining the effort to save the company is, hands down, the smart thing, and the right thing, to do. Your colleagues, however, may see it differently. Don't be surprised if you receive a chilly reception from some coworkers, and unbridled hostility from others. Face it, some employees will consider your decision to volunteer to help the company as a betrayal of the "us" versus "them" paradigm. They will assume that your choice is merely a cynical, calculated attempt to save your job at their expense.

Instead of withdrawing from your colleagues or acting defensive, be ready to respond by stepping up your interaction with the group. You want to stay as connected as possible to your colleagues. How can you do that? Immediately upon being selected to join the effort to right the company, meet with colleagues to explain why you volunteered and what responsibilities you have been assigned. Invite your coworkers to also become involved. Ask for their ideas and suggestions about what they think the company should do to move forward. If a coworker does present an idea, tell your manager and ask her to personally thank the employee for his contribution.

You want your coworkers to understand that you didn't volunteer because you want to showcase yourself or advance your career. Your motivation is simple—you want to help the company survive so that you and they have jobs. So say something like, "The company is trying to get to a different place, and my effort here is in the interest of all of us."

Stay positive, and try to keep as many of your colleagues as possible feeling positive. Despite your best efforts, some coworkers will still feel that you have sold out. Expect one or two people to openly challenge your reason for participating. Every company has, well, let's just say, people like that. Don't react to them. Their problem is that they are small-minded and short-sighted.

Your choice may also cause more subtle changes in your relationships with people. You may even lose some friendships. The only thing you can do is remember the fundamental reason you got involved: Your success, your paycheck, and the success and paychecks of all your coworkers really do depend on the company's success.

70. Help Your Manager Communicate Better

Communication is the key to being a successful manager. Yet, many managers simply don't communicate well with the people reporting to them. Consequently, the manager struggles to understand why his programs always hit roadblocks. If you have a good, honest relationship with your manager, you may be able to help him be a better communicator, which in turn will win you his gratitude and help keep your job.

Everyone has a blind spot about himself. It can be something he does, or says, or a way that he behaves that he is unaware of. The way you remove that blind spot is to have someone who cares about you expose it to you. Because you trust that person, ideally you are then motivated to address the issue. Of course, that assumes that you want to learn, grow, and develop as an individual, and are capable of accepting feedback with a positive attitude.

Managers are no different when it comes to having a professional blind spot. For many, it is the inability to communicate with employees. As one of those employees, you know that your manager's message isn't getting through, because you listen to and see how your coworkers respond. The question, then, is how do you tell your boss that his communication skills are more along the lines of George W. Bush than Ronald Reagan? Very carefully. If you choose to intervene, you are truly a brave, courageous, and bold individual. Okay, perhaps not. Maybe you're getting involved because you realize that it is the only way to increase the department's production, which, of course, is the best way to help everyone keep his or her job. Good for you. Just be tactful.

Actually, before saying a word to your boss, check with your colleagues to make sure you are reading their reactions correctly. If you are, step back and carefully consider the strength of your relationship with your manager. If it is good and you know that he is open to constructive feedback, take the plunge. Remember, you are providing unsolicited feedback. So approach your manager in a humble, authentic manner. And keep in mind that your whole purpose is to help him be successful. The good news is that most managers want to know how to be more effective in their job.

During a one-on-one meeting with your manager, don't just blurt out, "Harry, you have a problem." Regardless of how sound your relationship is, that won't go over well. Instead, make it clear that you think he is doing a fine job and that you fully support him. Then, add something like, "But I have this feeling that the team could use more support from you and acknowledgment when things are going well. Maybe you could talk to the folks a little more and, you know, say hello or stop by people's desks to chat for a moment."

Stop there. You don't want to venture any farther out on the limb. The ball is now in your manager's court. Chances are he will respond by saying he didn't realize people wanted more attention. In fact, don't be surprised if your manager extends the conversation and reveals some things that he wants to test on you. It may also open the door to discussions about management philosophy, or other office issues. Sharing those conversations with you is a great sign. It means your manager has heard your feedback and is taking you into his confidence. And that's like coating your job in Kevlar.

71. Listen to Gossip

Always be willing to listen to gossip, but never become a gossiper. Having an anti-gossip policy will almost certainly tamp down the amount of gossip floating around your office. But it probably won't completely eliminate it. That's because, for some people, gossip is like that second donut you eat—you don't need it, you know you shouldn't have it, but you just can't stop yourself from wolfing it down.

Gossip differs from rumor in that gossip tends to be about people and includes information that is true or factual. A rumor is usually about a thing, and generally you would be lucky to find even a trace amount of truth in it.

People gossip for several reasons. Some people are gossipers for the same reason people watch soap operas and reality television, or read the supermarket tabloids. They want to know that other people have problems or are screwing up their lives far worse than they are. Consequently, they feel like they have it so much more together.

Yet, by its very nature, gossip is destructive. For starters, employees who gossip are less productive. They usually create a huge distraction that incubates an atmosphere of distrust.

The real attraction of gossip is that you know a secret which no one else is privy to. And that means you have power. But the only way to exercise that power is to tell someone else the secret. But of course, the moment you whisper the secret into the other person's ear, you lose the power and a whole lot more. When you tell the secret, you think you are showing your power when, in fact, all you are doing is telling everyone that you are an unreliable and untrustworthy gossip. Ironic, isn't it?

So, how can listening to gossip help you keep your job? While you shouldn't and don't condone gossip, paying attention to what is being said around your office will help you keep your job because it is based on fact. And knowing who is saying what, gives you tremendous insight into another level of office politics. So, if someone chooses to share gossip with you, listen. Just don't respond. Coworkers dish to you because they know you don't gossip. By staying mum, you become the most politically savvy person in the organization.

But what do you do if someone gossips about you? Confront them. Go the person spreading gossip about you and tell them what you have heard they are saying and that you would like it stopped immediately.

What should you do if you hear something about an employee that you think your manager should know? Remember, gossip does contain some facts. Still, tread carefully. Unless you think the information you have heard poses a real threat to your department or the company, don't say anything. Why not? Because sharing gossip with your manager can backfire on you, big time. Say you have a piece of information you think the manager should know. With your stellar reputation of not indulging in gossip, you think it will give you some special standing with your manager. So you go in to your boss and say, "Hey, Sarah, I just wanted to let you know that Mary might be about to leave. I heard she is looking around, and I thought you might want to know to go try and save her." You think you did your boss a service. But your boss is thinking, "Man, what a vulture. Who else would he sell out?"

A wise person once said, don't do anything that you wouldn't want to see on the front page of the *New York Times*. The same goes for sharing a piece of gossip. If you are willing to say what you heard to his or her face, then go ahead. So, if you have a problem with one of your teammates who isn't pulling his weight, you can go to your manager. But ask for the teammate in question to be present. You will retain your reputation for not being a gossip, and your manager will see you as an upstanding, straight-shooting employee.

72. Call Attention to Problems

When business is off significantly, it is important to bring problems affecting the performance of the team or department to your manager's attention. But before bursting into your manager's office railing about inefficiencies in the work process, talk to your colleagues to make sure everyone agrees. The idea is to work together as a team to streamline the organization, increase productivity, and save jobs.

Managers are not always aware of waste in production and performance. If no one complains, most managers simply assume things are running smoothly. Let's say, for instance, a team is running a report that is no longer necessary. No one is asking for the report. No one is using the data generated by the report. Yet, every day or week, the report is produced. It's not uncommon in business to have routine activities like reports take on a life of their own. Or maybe running the report is a colleague's main duty, which is why you should confer with coworkers before calling it to your manager's attention. After all, you don't want to be the guy who is seen as sacrificing someone else's job in order to save his own.

Together with your coworkers, identify unnecessary routine reports or activities that, if discontinued, would save the company money and make the department more productive. Before going to your manager, thoroughly study and understand the process under review. Look at it from different angles so you can hold a constructive conversation with your manager and offer ideas. Then, as a group, bring the issue to your manager's attention. You want to go as a group, or representing the group, because that makes it a win/win situation for everyone. More importantly, no one looks like he is going after another worker's job to save his own.

If an obvious business process or administrative function within your department is a problem and no one wants to address it, you may have to go it alone. Approach the issue by saying something to your boss like, "Nancy, we have a series of training courses that have a low attendance and just really aren't as important now as when business was booming. I think it's in the department's best interest to suspend the classes for now."

Utilize Tip 73: Bring at Least One Solution, and don't stop there. Suggest dropping the three-course series in favor of a new, more relevant, single class on How to Be More Effective and Efficient in Your Job. If your colleagues really don't need any courses, explain that to your manager so that she recognizes the value and benefit to the department of eliminating the program.

Another problem might be an activity that is wasting your time. Again, approach the manager with a logical answer to the situation. Explain how the activity takes you away from doing higher value work for the department. Give your manager tangible details like, "I have to do a report and update every week that takes up twenty percent of my time and adds no value to the department, when I could be spending that time with my customers."

Your manager may not agree with you, but in any case, she will be impressed with the mature, rational approach you took and realize that you are an asset to the company.

BE CAREFUL WITH COWORKERS

Be wary of going to your manager alone with a coworker problem, especially when business is bad. For too many things can go wrong, even if everyone in the department acknowledges that the coworker is best described as the hindquarters of an equine. Ironically, if you approach your manager alone, there is a chance that your manager may come away wondering if you aren't the real problem.

The best way to deal with a problem person is as a group. Together, ask the person why he or she is not pitching in, or spreading rumors, or causing conflicts. Ask what is keeping him or her from being a team player. If that gets you nowhere, the group has at least cleared the air. Then, together, decide whether or not you want to bring the issue to your manager.

73. Bring at Least One Solution

When you approach your manager with a problem, make sure you also have a remedy. Managers caught in a downsizing environment are usually stretched pretty thin. Where she was normally responsible for ten or twenty employees, the number of direct report employees can more than double during difficult economic times. So the last thing your manager wants to hear is someone complaining about a problem who has expended no energy working on a solution.

On the other hand, managers covet employees who provide suggestions, options, and answers to issues that arise. And unlike their colleagues who simply dump more trouble on their manager's desk, the I-have-an-idea employee stands a far greater chance of staying on the payroll. If you're the manager, whom to keep shouldn't be a difficult decision.

The obvious question for you, then, is figuring out the best way to resolve a specific problem. Actually, there are a couple of methods. Each way, however, requires that you are a self-starter who is more interested in solving an issue than in claiming credit. Remember, you can accomplish a lot more if you don't care about who gets the credit. Anyway, sharing credit is good for you, your coworkers, and the company. And don't worry, your manager will know that you worked your butt off bringing the parties together to forge an agreement. But before you can solve a problem, you have to first break it down and:

✔ Define it.
✔ Analyze the current situation.

✔ Understand what can happen if the current situation isn't changed.
✔ Understand how the problem is already affecting the group.

As you embark on the journey to consensus, remember the words of that famous philosopher, Paul Simon, who said, "One man's ceiling is another man's floor." Understanding that two people or groups of people can experience the same event in totally dissimilar ways will help you get through some very frustrating moments as you work toward a solution.

Convene a meeting of everyone with skin in the game or, as they are known in business lexicon, the stakeholders. Along with their determined points of view, these people also possess the information that you need to break down the dilemma and begin the heavy lifting of brainstorming and negotiating. Lay out the options. You can:

✔ Stay with the status quo and not resolve the problem.
✔ Address one or more parts of the issue to see if it changes anything.

The back-and-forth will take time, so be patient. And always talk in terms of "we" rather than "I," so no one feels that he or she is being blamed or demonized. Finally, have the group settle on a resolution and how to best implement it. Then bring the solution into a meeting with your manager.

Your manager may support the group's work, but chances are she will want to do some tweaking with the proposed solution. Don't fight minor changes. Yes, you did the hard work and probably had to stroke a few egos along with way. But there may be matters you don't know about that may require your manager to massage your plan. So don't dig your heels in. Be flexible. In fact, your manager's tinkering with your plan is a good sign. It means she is willing to put a personal stamp on it, thus increasing the chances of the plan being implemented.

For you, the game was won by simply showing up in your manager's office with a problem and a solution. It shows your manager that you are interested in the greater good of the company and not just your own interest. She will recognize that you took the time to do the research, organize the parties, and form a consensus. If nothing else, you have established yourself as a leader and someone any manager would want on her team.

74. Know How Your Company Views Itself

Every company has a clear self-image, a specific business strategy, and defined goals that it professes to embody. Some companies call these things a mission statement, while others refer to them as a vision. In either case, you, as an employee who wants to keep your job, must understand and identify with the organization's stated purpose and noble intent.

Companies use mission/vision statements to help employees identify with where the business is going and its purpose in the world. The statements craft a compelling image of an achievable future that transcends words and stirs the imagination. But the best go beyond even that. Those mission/vision statements inspire people to believe that being part of the organization makes them special, even unique. That is why employees wear ball caps, T-shirts, and jackets emblazoned with the company logo. They are proud to belong to such a well-intentioned, highly respected company.

But for a mission/vision statement to accomplish all of that, it must represent something that is possible and achievable. For instance, medical science has spent decades trying to find a cure for cancer. And while a cure has yet to be found, people continue working in the field because they believe that the mission/vision is possible and achievable. Moreover, the workers are fulfilled in their jobs because they feel they are doing honorable, important work.

If you are employed by a company that is in a business tailspin, the best way to protect your job is to sign on to and directly attach yourself to the company's mission/vision statement. When business is down, the company wants you and every other employee to adapt the grand ideals of the mission/vision statement to your job. In essence, management wants you to make the vision a workplace reality. So, the easiest way to convince your manager that you are worth keeping around is to live the mission/vision statement in your job and your dealings with coworkers. You can do that by listening to and learning about management's business strategy and translating it to your department or job. Then, develop an action plan that responds to the strategy and bring it to your manager. If nothing else, it will show your manager that you understand how the company's vision relates to your job or department. In addition, you are saying to senior executives that you identify with what the company is trying to accomplish. And that should help you keep your job.

Some aspects of a company's social culture may differ from department to department. Each group develops a set of beliefs, values, and behaviors that, over time, become embedded into the department's daily work life. The values form the department's unwritten rules and norms of what is acceptable and unacceptable behavior. Culture, even at the department level, is very powerful. Whether or not you adapt to a group's established culture will determine if you keep your job.

In general, a department's culture is dictated by the manager. If the manager acts a certain way, then everyone else in the department is expected to follow suit. For instance, if the manager makes it a point to treat every employee, regardless of rank, with respect and dignity, then the department culture will demand that everyone do the same. The same holds true about arriving to work on time, working hard during the day, and helping each other out when you can. Sometimes the culture extends outside of work, with office parties, other social events, or even personal emergencies. Parts of a department's culture can be articulated, but mostly new employees learn a culture by taking cues from their environment and by modeling their behavior from watching the way their colleagues behave. Clearly, it is necessary to understand and adapt to your department's culture.

75. Become the Face of the Company in the Community

Almost every corporation has philanthropic goals. Businesses affiliate themselves with specific charities or causes to help people in the broader community. The actual work—the planning, organizing, and getting people to contribute—is usually done by employees who, for whatever reason, get involved and volunteer their time.

Being identified as an employee engaged in the company's charity work is not only personally fulfilling but a great way to protect your job in hard times. Why? Because giving of yourself to help others helps you stand out in the best way possible. Your peers will respect you, and management will note your leadership skills.

Getting involved with the company's charity work—orchestrating a fund-raising event, organizing a community cleanup day, getting people to participate in a blood drive, serving meals on a holiday—shows your manager that you're not just a clock puncher but someone who is invested in the company and cares enough about its image in the community to get involved. You are showing, among other things, compassion and leadership.

In fairness, becoming part of the company's charity work is not for everyone. And that's fine. Some people come to volunteering more naturally. But if you choose to join in, be committed. If you're not, people will see through your charade and consider your effort calculated and political. You may surprise yourself. What may start out feeling uncomfortable can turn into a fantastic, fulfilling experience. You will never realize how good you can feel about yourself until you go out of your way to help someone else.

Jill experienced that feeling when she volunteered to help a company-sponsored charity. The opportunity came during a staff meeting. The company's senior vice president mentioned that the company had asked him to spearhead an event for a well-known organization that worked with dying children. In truth, he didn't exactly sound thrilled with the extra work.

Jill saw her opportunity. She loved the charity's work and decided this was the opportunity she was looking for. Immediately after the meeting, she went to the senior vice president's office. She told her boss that she loved the charity's work and was excited about helping out. In fact, if he wanted, she would take responsibility for organizing the entire event. The vice president, who already had a plateful of work, was happy to oblige.

In the ensuing weeks, Jill worked on the arrangements on her own time. She got to know the people at the charity, set up a committee, planned the event, and took care of all the details. The event was a tremendous success, bringing in more than $300,000 in contributions.

Of course, the credit for the event's success went to Jill's boss. And that was fine with her. After all, her senior vice president knew who did the work. And the administrators from the charity couldn't say enough good things about her. But even more importantly, Jill felt really great about helping kids who had been dealt such a rotten hand.

By stepping up and volunteering, Jill got a triple win. She made new friends at the charity, with whom she continues to work. By taking the burden off the senior vice president, Jill was now on his radar screen as someone looking to learn, trustworthy, and very capable of handling more responsibility. And if the time comes when jobs are on the line at the company, do you think Jill has anything to worry about? Not if her senior vice president has anything to say about it.

76. Represent the Company with Style and Grace

No matter the circumstances, regardless of the time or place, you always represent your company. If you want to keep your job, make sure you do so with the utmost style and grace.

Your public deportment is a reflection of your company and its standards. Even at a nonbusiness event, be mindful that you are, at that moment, the face of the company in the community.

And people really do expect a certain type of behavior and a good measure of sophistication, as well as an appealing physical presentation, from professionals in particular fields. A doctor friend tells the story about a patient who came to him and requested that the doctor's colleague not perform her child's operation. The doctor, knowing his colleague to be a highly skilled surgeon, asked why not? The patient said, "Did you see the examination room? It was a mess. And did you see the way he looked? He has a coffee stain on his white coat." The messy room and the physician's sloppy appearance didn't fit with the patient's image of what a good surgeon should look like.

How well you dress and present yourself clearly influences peoples' perception and image of your profession. It may not be fair. After all, this unkempt doctor is actually a gifted surgeon. Yet, you must look the part of a person in your profession or risk turning off prospective clients, which certainly will put your job in jeopardy. Consequently, you must make sure that you dress to fit your industry's image. For example, if you are in the corporate world, dark-colored business suits are de rigueur for work.

That said, it is also true that different industries have different definitions of style and grace. The button-down style of Goldman Sachs probably wouldn't work in the more laid back, looser work environment of Google. So, make sure the way you represent the company fits with the company's corporate image. Some companies are engaging, while others are more stolid.

It is very important that you understand exactly how the company expects you to act. But knowing what you can and cannot say is equally vital. The degree to which you can reveal information about your company depends on several things. For example, people who work for publicly owned businesses usually have more latitude because the business's books are open. But if you work for a privately held concern, the reins on what you may say publicly are held much tighter.

There are also legal concerns. Many businesses are regulated by the federal government, such as the health-care industry. The Healthcare Insurance Portability and Accountability Act of 1996 prohibits people working in health care from talking about or revealing medical facts about patients. Since the insider trading scandals of the 1990s, the Securities and Exchange Commission has regulated the type of information people working on Wall Street, or for brokerage companies, are allowed to tell clients.

Representing your company with style and grace finally comes down to being comfortable in your job and knowing how the company would like you to act in public. As a professional, that should mean you present yourself as an honest and confident member of your organization.

77. Refer Good People to the Company

Referring good people to work for your company will earn you points with management and help you keep your job. Finding talented people shows management that you are invested in the long-term success of the company.

Referring people can be a little tricky. The big issue is finding the line between referring and campaigning for your candidate. Also, you should think long and hard about whom you suggest. Whoever the person, if he gets the job he will represent your judgment—good or bad—in your manager's mind. And that is probably why you never want to throw the names of relatives or friends into the mix.

So, how do you get your manager interested in a prospect? First of all, don't go overboard with the praise. You know the person and his work, but you don't know how he will perform during an interview. Setting your manager's expectations too high may doom a less than brilliant interviewee. Try a softer sell like, "I know John from my last job, and I think he did a good job. We weren't good friends or anything like that. I've asked him, and he said he would be interested in talking with you. Here is the name of his boss, if you would like to talk to her as well. I think he's at least worth talking to." You have presented everything in a solid, but measured way. The rest is up to your manager.

Let's say you do have a friend who is perfect for a job with your company. Again, give a low-key assessment and let your boss decide. You can say something like, "I have a friend who is looking for a job, and I think he would be a strong candidate for the position that we have open. But then again, I think you should make that call." Give the manager your friend's name and telephone number and walk away.

If your company is in trouble, chances are the person you refer isn't going to jump ship to join you. That's fine. You still garner points with the bosses because you showed an interest in helping the company succeed. And who knows, next year after the company rebounds, the individual may be willing to reconsider.

GET INVOLVED IN THE HIRING PROCESS

Another way to stand out and keep your job is to become involved in your company's hiring process. Most companies have a multitiered hiring process that starts with a search committee and several layers of people who screen and cull the prospects. How do you get the job? Pure, raw initiative. Volunteer for a post as soon as you hear the process has begun. You may start out on a committee that defines the job. Or your committee may be charged with writing the job description, defining candidate qualifications, and determining salary range, among other duties.

As you gain experience, your responsibilities may expand to include screening and then interviewing. In any case, being involved in the process raises your profile and shows that you are committed to the company beyond your job.

78. Take Care of Your Customers

No matter the market or industry, the old business axiom, "People do business with people they trust," still holds true. When you show a customer, through your actions, words, and deeds, that you have their best interests at heart, the customer will trust you. And then you can begin to build a "beautiful friendship," or at least a good business relationship. The way you lay the foundation for that relationship is through your sincerity, the quality of your work, and the feedback you offer. You want the customer to know that they are the most important person in the relationship. Don't be shy about saying so. And then back it up with your actions and deeds.

Show that your interest is genuine by telling your client why you like working with them. But even more important than words are your actions. Deliver on your promises. You should also make yourself aware of the issues facing your customer, especially when it comes to her client. Use your knowledge of the industry to give your customer a "heads up" about issues that can negatively affect their business or them personally. And then be discreet with that information. Finally, honor relationships within your client's organization, and always be professional. It really isn't much more complicated than that.

Dealing with a new client sometimes means you have to clean up a mess left by your predecessor. Roy Roper fell into that situation. He inherited a *Fortune* 500 client, a major airline with 50,000 employees. The client was threatening to leave the company because he didn't feel Roper's company understood the level of sophistication the business required. Roper took over the account and met with an airline executive. He sat down and talked to the person. Roper explained that he really wanted to understand what the client thought was missing in the relationship. What did the client feel that he wasn't getting, and what was making him unhappy? Roper listened and took notes. Then he went to work determined to deliver everything the client wanted.

He started by developing an action plan. It highlighted every issue and concern voiced by the client. Then Roper wrote down how he would address each of those problems. He also scheduled a regular monthly meeting with the client. At each meeting, Roper listened to his client's concerns and used the business plan to monitor their progress. He was careful never to promise what he knew he couldn't deliver. Roper turned around the account by understanding what was important to the client. In time the client came to believe and trust that Roper could make a difference in providing the service the client sought.

"I made the customer an individual," Roper said. "So, although he worked for a 50,000-person airline, I made him my customer. From a situation where he was very unhappy, we became friends."

79. Understand Your Client's Company Culture

If you want to be successful in today's global economy, you must be aware of the cultural differences in the way business is conducted. And that rule applies whether your client is in Hong Kong or Hoboken. In either case, being culturally aware can help you keep your job if you invest the time to learn about different cultures and share that information with your team or company.

For years, American business people were anything but understanding when it came to dealing with their counterparts from around the globe. As the biggest economic engine in the world, American businesses called all the shots. You do realize that the term "ugly American" had nothing to do with our looks?

Today, thanks to the global marketplace and the rise of Japanese, Chinese, and Indian economies, American business has changed its point of view. Executives now realize that unless they learn to respect people and their cultures, they will not earn the business. So, more and more companies are holding classes and training seminars about the different people and cultures around the world. Sometimes, however, the best lessons come from experience.

For instance, the first time Emmy Miller went to Austria on business, she learned a little about how business was done in Europe. Her client sent a car to pick her up at the airport and take her to the hotel. The driver informed her that he would wait for her to freshen up before touring her around Vienna.

"He was saying to me, 'You can't work with me unless you understand my world,'" says Miller, president of Liberty Business Strategies, based in Ardmore, Pennsylvania.

Her client was happy that Miller agreed to try some of the local food, and even more thrilled when she displayed her knowledge of Austrian wines.

While giving a presentation in Asia to a diverse group of people from China, Australia, and Malaysia, Alex was using hand gestures. As he spoke, Alex would turn the palms of his hands facing up and occasionally point to people in the audience. Alex became aware that a group of Malaysian businessmen were not participating in the presentation. In fact, the entire group was staring blankly straight ahead. Only later did Alex learn that his hand gestures had offended the Malaysian contingent. It was explained that in Malaysian culture a person never points and that their hands are always presented palms facing down.

In Japan, it is considered inappropriate to publicly confront another person or force him to take a position or stand. The Japanese culture minimizes the importance of the individual in favor of the group. So people rarely are challenged in public. If your company wants to do business successfully abroad, employees need to know about the effect hand gestures and debating can have in some cultures.

But even here at home, you must understand that every business has its own culture that you must learn and respect. For instance, some companies are all business. Their managers and executives are not interested in developing any relationship beyond the transaction. If you try to force a relationship, you will lose their business.

The culture in other companies is to keep you away from decision makers. It could take months or years for you to navigate though a gauntlet of secretaries and assistants until you get an audience with the person you want. It is important, then, to find out the particular culture of the company you want to do business with, and what are its norms.

When you finally do get through, take that information back to your colleagues. Explain what you went through, and give them all the unspoken rules that you have learned. Spreading your knowledge and information throughout your department, enlightening your coworkers about the unique cultural norms of your clients will make you all the more valuable to your manager.

80. Know Your Customer's Customer

It's a given that you should know as much about your client's business and professional needs as possible. But if you really want to endear yourself to a client, put in the time to learn about your client's client.

The more you know about your client's end customer, the more valuable you become to your client. How does that help you keep your job? Well, how often can your client say that you know as much about his end customer as his own staff? Probably not often. So, you can bet that your client will be so impressed with how much you are invested in her success, that she will crow about it to your boss. And that is always a good thing when it comes to helping you keep your job.

To understand the relationship between your client and his customer, you have to spend as much time doing research as you would if you were job hunting. In other words, know it inside out. Then ask your client questions about how he uses your product or service. If your client wonders why you want to know, explain that part of your job is helping him be successful. And the best way to do that is by knowing how his company uses your product or service to assist the end customer. With that information in hand, you will also be able to suggest new or different ways for your client to employ your product or service for other customers, or simply as a tool to market the company.

A well-known international computer company instructs its employees on the value of knowing the customer's customer, by inviting its customers to speak at staff meetings. At one meeting, a customer told the group that, after years of dealing with the company, it was clear to him the computer giant was far more valuable to him if the design engineers and salespeople know his customers and, through the design, help him satisfy the end user's needs.

That same international company was commissioned to build an operating system for Disney, the movie and entertainment park conglomerate. Before pencil was set to paper to draft a design, the two sides met to discuss what the attraction the computer would control was expected to do. The people building the operating system realized that they were not just selling technology. They were helping the Walt Disney Company to create an experience for its customers'—both kids and parents—entertainment.

The beauty of knowing your customer's customer is that everyone involved reaps the rewards. Your manager is happy. Your client is happy. The end customer is happy. And for you, that all adds up to keeping your job.

81. Enhance Your Workplace

It may not be in the cards for you to pull off that one, hugely impressive feat that helps save the company. Maybe you can't convince your coworkers to pull together through change, or make your boss look like manager of the year. Sometimes you can save your job simply by doing lots and lots of little things that make you indispensable.

What kinds of things? How about developing a flexible work schedule for your department? Granted, on the surface, creating a flexible work schedule really doesn't shout out, "Keep this guy/girl on the payroll." But if you look beyond the surface, a flexible work schedule can do a lot for the company's bottom line and employee morale.

In today's hectic world of dual-income families, it helps if one partner has some flexibility when it comes to his or her work schedule. Employees with children face challenges every day. There are the daily concerns about dropoff and pickup times. If the weather is bad, many schools delay opening until 10 A.M. For companies with rigid hours, it usually means the employee will take the day off. But with a flexible schedule, the parent can stay home, take his child to school, and then report to work. Plus, a parent worried about a child, regardless of the reason, is not a very productive employee. Other employees may need to check on elderly parents. And with all the other demands, an employee has no time for a doctor or dentist visit.

When employees are on a flexible schedule, they can avoid the frustration of sitting in rush-hour traffic, which means that they arrive at work in a better frame of mind and ready to work. So, having a flexible schedule helps employees cope with an already busy day. And when the company extends itself for its workforce, morale soars and workers usually show their gratitude by not leaving. Not only does the company have a happy and indebted worker, but it saves a bundle of money. It's Business 101. For example, a large, well-known national insurance company estimates it costs $17,000 to hire and bring a new employee up to speed. If that employee performs poorly or leaves, the meter clocks out at $30,000.

There are other things you can suggest to management to help retain employees, like making outside services available that can recommend auto repairs shops, doctors, and other everyday needs to help them save time. You can propose allowing employees to trade a raise or bonus for the right to work from home one day a week. Again, in bad weather employees can log in from home. Also, if the office computer system crashes, the person working in her home office isn't affected. A surgical practice in a large city hospital always has one employee from its billing department working at home every day. If the office computer goes down, most of the bills for that day will still go out.

Other recommendations that cost the company very little but will give a big payback are things like putting antiseptic handwash on each desk during cold and flu season, encouraging employees to take a short stroll every few hours, and providing a quiet area where an employee can concentrate. To help people cope with the stress that accompanies an economic downturn, add some plants to the office and teach basic relaxation techniques. None of these ideas are big enough or game-changing enough on their own to save your job. But the fact that each suggestion shows that you have an interest in your coworkers and that you are thinking about the company's bottom line, will not go unnoticed.

82. Be Prepared to Talk about Your Project

Having an elevator speech ready to promote your project or department is a good strategy any time. But when business is down, it is critical. A well-practiced, finely honed elevator speech may save your project, and your job.

Your project-saving elevator speech should take no more than two minutes, or roughly the time it takes to ride a couple of floors. Unlike the pep-talk elevator speech in Tip 100, where you choose what to say, members of the core team or the department manager decides what message you will deliver. That is because the elevator speech in Tip 100 is a promotion of your positive, personal brand. The elevator speech in this tip is a unified sales pitch. So the department manager, either alone or in concert with the core team, selects three or four of the project's strongest points. If the pitch were in writing those would be the bullet points. The idea is to have everyone on the team highlighting the same, positive points because the message has to be consistent in order for it to work.

The elevator speech should be well rehearsed. Still, try to make it sound casual, like small talk. Let's say you meet a senior manager on the elevator who asks what your team is working on. Your response should sound something like this: "We're really excited about our project because we know that it will help the organization bolster the bottom line. What we found was that our project can . . ." then rattle off your bullet points. If the question instead is about what you are doing, start off by saying something like, "I'm working with a great group of people focused on . . ." and give the talking points.

A word of caution here: Whatever points you choose to promote, they must be legitimate. Never lie or even exaggerate because you think it sounds better. If you get caught lying, you won't just ruin your brand. You will destroy your teammates' brands and the project itself. There should be no wiggle room whatsoever in your talking points.

NEVER BE NEGATIVE

Even more important than having a good elevator speech is never allowing anyone to hear you say anything negative about your team, project, or department. Every team member must be on board with the project, enthusiastically sounding the same themes. It's okay to talk about uphill battles as long as you follow that with how the team is working through those challenges and knocking down problems one at a time.

83. Take a Promotion Without the Pay Increase

The possibility exists that your tireless efforts and dedication to helping the company navigate through turbulent financial waters will see you rewarded with the offer of a job promotion, without a salary increase. With the offer of a promotion on the table, it would seem that your job does not require saving. Not so fast. Before you give your thumbs up or thumbs down to the offer, think through all the permutations.

From the company standpoint, the most Machiavellian scenario for the offer of a promotion—and therefore the least likely—is that your current position is going to be eliminated because of downsizing. Your manager knows that losing you—and your positive, team-oriented attitude—would create a huge hole in the department. You are being presented with the opportunity to move up, more or less, to keep you on the team. If you decline the promotion because it doesn't come with a higher salary or enhanced benefits, you should expect to receive an envelope with a pink slip inside. The company loses a great asset—you—but saves a salary. If you take the job, it means even more responsibilities and longer hours.

All that said, it is probably best for you to take the bump up in position for a couple of reasons. First of all, more than likely you are already juggling more work than what is laid out in your job description. So you may as well have the fancy title to go with it. On the plus side, you will rack up even more points with your manager. How could you not? You are showing that you are aware of the world beyond your job by understanding the ramifications of the overall business environment of your company. You are still a great team player who is doing everything you can to help the company weather the financial crisis. And you have the good sense not to affront your manager or the company by rejecting a promotion at a time when plenty of other people are being furloughed. Really, does it make any sense at all to snub your boss?

There is one other reason to take the promotion without any remorse: Is it something that, under normal circumstances, you would covet? If the position, or just a promotion, is something that was among the goals for your career this year, why hesitate? Take it and cross off "Earn a promotion" from your to-do list. Sure, it would be nice to get a promotion and a nice chunk of cash to go with it. But remember, people are losing their jobs. And money, really and truly, isn't everything. If by taking the promotion you reap some psychological or emotional reward, then that's enough. If the job is the dream of a lifetime, even at the same pay rate and with no additional vacation time, you are being compensated in other ways.

Also, take the promotion with an eye to the future. No matter what happens, you have earned the position and title. Both will work for you in advancing your career when the company gets back on its feet. Gaining the promotion will also present you with the opportunity to do great things as you advance. So, no matter how you look at it, no matter what conditions you accepted it under, the promotion is an investment in your career.

Any business coach or consultant will tell you that, as an employee, whenever you deal with your employer you want to reach a win/win outcome. Sometimes what you see as a win won't be recognized that way by other people. But if the business circumstances, personal situation, and outcome satisfy you as a win, take the deal.

84. Be Willing to Defer Some Rewards

Sometimes, all it takes to save your job is to act mature and keep your temper in check. Let's say that your performance over the past year has been stellar. You are easily exceeding all the goals set during your annual evaluation with your manager. By all standards, you should receive a handsome salary raise and the maximum year-end bonus.

Then, one morning, your manager visits your cubicle with some bad news, some good news, and more bad news. The bad news is sales are down, the economy stinks, and there may be layoffs. The good news is that because you're so good at your job, work hard, are a team player, have outstanding leadership qualities, and make a cup of coffee to die for, your job is iron-clad safe. As for the other dose of bad news, you won't be getting a raise or bonus this year.

Before you dump your cup of coffee on your manager's lap, take a deep breath and think about how you want to respond. What image of yourself do you want to project to your manager? Sure you're upset. But unless the last time you read a newspaper or watched a news broadcast was during the Clinton Administration, you had to know that the decompressing economy was going to affect your company. So really, should you feel blindsided by your manager's announcement? And at a time when people would gladly trade their raises, bonuses, or both to stay employed, do you have a reason to complain? And if you recall, during your manager's visit, he wasn't asking you to forgo your raise, and waive your bonus.

Nevertheless, how you react to the news will go a long way toward defining your future as part of your manager's team, as well as whether you remain part of the company. If you scream and shout at your manager about how lousy the company is for stiffing you out of money you earned, the only thing you are doing is showing your manager that he has one more angry, soon-to-be less productive malcontent to supervise.

Or here's an idea—you can take the high road. By being emotionally mature and utterly pragmatic—remember that you're not getting the money anyway—you can make the bad news work for you. Tell your manager that you are disappointed that raises and bonuses have been deferred, but that, in light of the current economic conditions, you understand. Then add something like, "I know this isn't something you are doing independently or enjoy doing. I appreciate that you have to do this as part of your job. And, hey, thanks for keeping me on board."

Don't be surprised if your manager is momentarily stunned. He is in the process of doing one of the least favorite managerial functions. And you can bet that the reception he has received from other employees hasn't been pleasant. So your moment of empathy will come as a surprise and impress your manager hard. You not only have just absolved him from being the bad person, but you thanked him for saving you from unemployment. Those bells you hear going off in the background are because you just hit the "Keep Your Job" jackpot.

By exercising emotional self-control, you have set yourself apart from everyone else in your department. In your manager's mind, you are a well-balanced, helpful employee who has the vision to see the wider picture beyond your job. And at a time when your manager needs all the helpful employees he can get, you have just moved to the front of the line. And all you did was make bad news work for you.

85. Accept the Combination of Two Jobs into One

A downturn in the nation's economy almost certainly means that your company will be searching for ways to save money. By staying alert to market trends, you can prepare for your company's fiscal frugality and keep your job.

The quickest way for a company to save money during a bad business cycle is to reduce the number of employees. Of course, those lucky enough to stay on will be expected to do more with less. Many times that means combining two jobs into one. As with deferred raises and bonuses, your manager will not be asking you to make the accommodation—she will be telling you.

So why wait for your boss to come knocking at your cubicle with an edict? Show leadership and creativity by getting ahead of the curve and developing a plan that may save your job or the job of a coworker.

At the first sign of a dip in the company's budgetary health, call a meeting of your coworkers. Enlisting your colleagues to work on a department plan is the best way to present your ideas to your manager. It will make you look like a team player and less like you are trying to save your own job. You also want your colleagues involved, because they will be the ones asked to implement your ideas. The more input they have early in the process, the less likely they are to balk later on.

Tell your coworkers that you see company-wide budget cuts coming that may cost a department member his or her job. Explain that the only way the group can hope to influence what happens to your department, is if you all work together to develop a plan. Ask people to come up with ideas. Among the areas to investigate are different ways for your team or organization to become more productive. Think about how work gets done in your department, and then write each team member's assignment. See if you can find time in your coworker's schedule for them to take on additional responsibilities.

Next, consider the possibility of realigning, redesigning, or redistributing the work within the department. You want to search for anything that will streamline the work process and increase the department's efficiency.

If your department has an unfilled position, figure out how the rest of the team can pick up the slack. Then, when job cuts come down, you may be able to exempt your department by pointing out to management that it is already operating one person short.

If you can't recruit your colleagues to help, then go to your manager alone. Lay out your ideas and thoughts, and never mention money. Instead, keep the conversation on how your department can weather the bad economy. Say something like, "I know times are tough, so I thought about how we can rearrange some of the responsibilities so that we can keep our team together. We may be able to collapse two jobs into one, and I would be happy to absorb some of these duties into my job." Always make sure to include your job and give yourself more work.

If your department doesn't have an unfilled position, suggest to your manager that, rather than lose someone, she could take in work from other departments. But if it is apparent that a job is going to be cut, don't mention any names. If someone has to go, you don't want it getting out that you named names. Moreover, your initiative and leadership in creating a plan has probably impressed your manager. You don't want to ruin that by suddenly having her question your motives.

86. Peer into the Future

When a business is spiraling downward, your manager and the entire management team are focused on the present and saving the company. And that is exactly what they should be doing. But somebody needs to be looking out over the next horizon, to the future, which is where you come in.

If there is any lesson to learn from the past few decades, it is that the cycle of change in business is growing shorter and moving faster. Yes, the management team has its hands full right now keeping the company viable. But that effort may be for naught if the company is unprepared for what is coming next. To make sure that your company stays attuned to its industry's evolution, suggest to your manager that you monitor and report on new, innovative business systems, concepts, and forward-thinking ideas. Volunteering to become your company's futurist—even if it is informal—can help you keep your job because management will recognize that you are a creative, out-of-the-box thinker who is interested in the organization. And if there is one kind of employee every company needs in today's hypercompetitive market, it is someone with a fresh approach and ideas.

But this won't be an easy add-on to your day job. The velocity of technological change is only going to increase in the coming years. The technology revolution in business started in the 1980s with the fax machine. People absolutely marveled how it could almost magically send a document from one office and print it out in an office across the country. And it only took minutes to do. That was just twenty-five years ago. Today, faxing is a business's third option for transmitting documents.

Even as your company struggles to survive, technology keeps thundering ahead. So, to stay abreast of the newest gadgets and software coming to market, start by reading industry publications. But that won't be enough. If you really want to stay informed, you will have to read everything from business-oriented technology magazines to nonbusiness, high-tech magazines. Also, consider attending seminars, lectures, and conventions dedicated to business and technology. And join business technology groups and online forums.

Technology and innovation will be how your company stays competitive in the future. Neither, however, will be sufficient if your organization doesn't have skilled workers. Yes, it is hard to think about finding, hiring, and retaining workers at a time when your company is contracting. But you had better start thinking about it if you want your organization to move forward. Sure, there will be plenty of people looking for work over the next several years. And there will be plenty of corporate suitors pursuing them. The question is, will those people possess the necessary training and skills the company needs? If not, what should a company be doing to identify those workers? And once the hiring is done, what can the company do to retain its staff members?

As you peer into the future, don't forget to look at the changes management will undergo. Some futurists say your manager will spend most of her time piecing together teams of staff members, freelancers, and consultants for project-by-project jobs. So she may also need to be retrained.

What will you likely find in the business of tomorrow that is part of business today? Change. It is a constant. And just like today, employees and managers who resist change will lose their jobs. The challenge, then, will be convincing people to learn to accept, if not welcome, change. The people who will flourish in the future will be similar to the people who keep their jobs today—they will be the employees who quickly accept and adjust to the ever-changing workplace.

Part IV

Master the Art
of Office Politics

The very thought of office politics turns off many people. But the fact is, office politics can be a good thing. Political dynamics are the way business operates. It is the currency that gets things done in the workplace. It's true that some office politics are destructive and dysfunctional. But contrary to what many people think, most office politics are above board and healthy. Whenever human beings form a group, there will always be a political dynamic. The challenge for employees is to understand how office politics work in their company. Once you do, you will be better prepared to engage, in a healthy way, and add value to your job. Plus, by participating you will learn about the destructive side of your office's politics and be better able to avoid it.

87. Make Office Politics Work for You

Before you can save your job using your office's political dynamic, you have to develop a keen self-awareness that not only allows you to understand what is going on, but to remain as balanced and objective as possible.

For most employees, office politics and balance and objectivity are all but mutually exclusive ideas. Instead, most employees rush to judgment, pigeonholing the political dynamic in one of three categories—good, bad, or indifferent. The side they choose is good, which makes whoever is on the other side indifferent or bad.

But the dynamic of office politics is much more involved and complex. To truly understand how it works, you must first be aware that during a bad business cycle the political dynamic becomes a free-for-all. Employees—let's call them stakeholders—are all trying their best to do their best. But with each stakeholder reacting to the poor business climate by doing what he or she thinks is right and necessary to save the company, and oh by the way, his or her job, a confusion of personal strategies is let loose.

Amidst this chaos, you can save your job, and probably a few others, by showing some leadership and not acting solely in your own best interest, thus separating yourself from the pack. Instead, you want to use the political dynamic to put together a strategy that will allow you to promote the interests of the company, your manager, and your department, as well as yourself. It will take some work. Why? Well, if you look out for yourself and the company, that may run counter to your manager's interest, and you don't want to do that. But if you cover your manager's and the company's concerns, you may leave out your coworkers and yourself.

Once you sort out everything, use the office's political dynamic to identify yourself as a positive force in your department and the company. Become known as someone who is balanced and objective and who helps people resolve conflicting interests with win/win solutions.

For instance, say you are sitting with your coworkers in the lunch room and a colleague starts talking about what he is going to do to protect his job. While what he says makes sense for him as an individual, it may conflict with the best interests of the team or your manager. In fact, your colleague's whole approach may come back and damage the entire department. Because you have established your brand as balanced and objective, you can point out to your coworker that what he wants to do may have severe implications for other people in the department. Suggest that he look for another way to have his needs satisfied, while having a positive impact on the other people in the department.

Using the office political dynamic to help save your job only works if you set yourself apart as a positive force in your department or company. People must know that you will be fair and honest when it comes to resolving problems and conflicts. Do that, and your manager will recognize you as someone who knows how to build bridges and create coalitions that help people have their needs met. Your manager will see you as someone who is vitally important to the well-being of your department and will do everything possible to protect your job.

88. To Have a Career, You Must Master Office Politics

Office politics can be a difficult course to navigate, even for the most savvy of employees. When business is going poorly, people immediately try to read whatever signs and signals are available. They want to know who is in, and who is out, so they can connect with the right people and get beyond the reach of any shrapnel from everyone else. It's disastrous enough getting identified as a member of the wrong crowd. But it is downright unforgivable to lose your job if you are collateral damage to another person's implosion.

All that said, cultivating a sense of who is hot and who is not takes years of experience with office politics to develop, including surviving a severe business downswing or two. Only the most astute office politicians can predict the way political alliances and coalitions will form, and sort out the interests and motives compelling those groups to band together. The seasoned political observer knows the individuals and their coalition's mates well enough to say if they are acting in their own interest, or out of a greater concern for the company. So, unless you fit that description, don't stake your job, and possibly your career, on a hunch. Listening to your gut, feeling it in your bones, or following your heart will only lead to trouble. Your brain should have the only vote.

That said, you will eventually have to learn to master your office's political dynamic if you don't want to have a limited career. Office politics is not just a fact of life; it is the way business gets done. And not all office politics is bad. It can be healthy and help the organization thrive and grow. But office politics can also be dysfunctional and destructive. And the deeper you delve into the political arena, the more complicated everything becomes. So, the key to saving your job in a tumultuous business cycle is staying neutral as long as possible, so you can garner information and watch how things are playing out. That said, you won't be allowed to just sit on the sidelines. If you try to completely ignore the politics going on around you, people will simply decide for themselves where you stand. Listen, ask questions, and when the time comes, hope you understand enough about your office's political dynamic to choose your side wisely.

As you make your choice, work through the implications of every decision. Once you decide to get involved, question whether you are doing it for yourself or for the company. Siding with the company is almost always a no-brainer. But your decision can't be based entirely on the company good. Why? Because there are multiple parties with different agendas and points of view, each saying theirs is right and more important. So you can take a stand about what is right for the company and still put your job and career in jeopardy with your manager. Your manager may not be siding with the company, because the company's position runs counter to his more immediate survival needs or self-interest.

And just like that, the political hot water reaches a boil. But really, how can you go wrong by backing the company? Because you still work for your manager, and he is in a prime position to undermine anything you try to do. So, how can you act in the best interest of both the company and your manager? If the two sides don't agree, talk to your manager to understand how you can help him be successful and still act in the best interest of the company. Your manager must believe that you are sincere and positive and not think that you are playing politics. It is a tough dance to master.

Getting involved in office politics can be dicey. Don't open your mouth until you have a handle on the intentions of the other parties involved. If you don't tread carefully, you may really be setting yourself up for serious political backlash.

89. Know When to Trust What Management Says

Keeping your job requires that you know when the company is telling you the truth. But how do you tease truth from—let's be generous—fiction? You can, with a strong dose of faith and a history lesson.

First, recognize that there are several reasons why the organization may withhold information. That doesn't make it right; it is just a fact of business. For instance, if you work for a publicly held company that is having a bad quarter, executives may feel that it is in the best interest of the company to delay releasing that data to avoid sinking the stock price.

At other times, the organization may simply manage information by not telling employees everything it knows. The company may believe that it is protecting its employees, who obviously are too fragile to hear bad news, by keeping them in the dark. But with so much information so readily available from so many sources today, that tack often backfires. It doesn't take long for employees to find out that the company's sales have fallen, its stock performance is off, and it has to cut expenses. Or worse, management waits until the last minute before releasing the bad news, catching everyone flat-footed. Suddenly, the company that a few days ago was saying everything was fine is now separating people from jobs like some out-of-control business threshing machine.

In the face of tough economic times, saving your job means listening closely to what management is actually doing. You can't protect your job if you don't know it needs protecting. Ask yourself if the message management is delivering is consistent with the reality people throughout the organization are experiencing. Are there any inconsistencies? Does what is being said make sense?

Then check the historical record. Look back at other public statements made by management. Did the company follow through with what it said it would do? If executives have consistently backed up what was said or promised, then there is reason to trust what they are saying now. But if management has a track record of saying one thing and doing another, there is no reason to give any credence to the latest proclamations.

It is important for any company to tell its employees the truth and follow through on what it promises. An honest and truthful management team earns trust and credibility with its employees. Lying, or unnecessarily withholding information from workers, will quickly destroy that relationship.

WHEN MANAGERS SPREAD RUMORS

A middle-level manager is often no better informed than her employees. Yet she is still expected to convey and support the information released by executives. Without complete information, the manager does what most people would do—make up their own meaning to complete the information. In doing so, she may add things that the company has no intention of honoring. Even worse is when a manager is told that there will be a 7 percent staff reduction, without being given a breakdown of where the cuts will come from. In an effort to keep her employees calm, she assures everyone that the department is in no danger. Then, a month later, she is informed to cut three people. The manager loses credibility and pays the price for management.

90. Be Aware of Trends and Changes in the Office

You have probably seen golfers tossing blades of grass into the air, or football field goal kickers studying the movement of those strips of cloth at the top of the goal posts. They're checking to see which way the wind is blowing so they can adjust their drive or kick accordingly. Well, you should be doing the same thing every day if you want to keep your job. No, you don't have to stand in the middle of the reception area flinging grass clippings in the air. But you do have to stay apprised of industry trends and subtle modulations in the pitch of your office and your business, especially in a slowing or flat economy. Rarely does a major change, like layoffs, occur without some sign or warning.

Tracking company and industry trends requires your eyes and ears to be wide open. It means staying in touch by reading industry newsletters and magazines, as well as tuning into business programs on radio and television. Log onto your computer and surf over to industry-based websites and check out blogs specific to your business. And don't be shy about contacting your counterparts at other industry companies. Place a few phone calls, exchange e-mails, or trade text messages with them. Be willing to barter information. Ask what they are hearing about business in general and specifically about your company. Sometimes people on the outside know more about what is quietly happening inside your company. In bad economic times, you have to keep your head up and your ears open. If you don't show an interest and know what is happening in your business, your manager will pick that up. If you want to be valuable to your group, you need to be tuned in to the business and industry. Doing your job well won't be enough to save you when the cuts come.

Sam did his job well. But he also paid close attention to how his company was changing. He realized that very quietly, more and more of the company's business was moving away from the local offices and into a more centralized location. Sam realized that if the trend continued, he would soon be unemployed. So he initiated contacts with the senior managers in his field at the company's national office and started coordinating his work with their work. Before long, he had made some friends in the national office who told him that the company's plan was to blend all the local offices into a series of regional hubs. Sam asked what he could do to ensure a smooth transition. The managers at the national office asked him if he would be interested in coordinating the closing of the local offices around him. Sam agreed.

Because Sam paid attention to the trends in the company, he was able to get out in front of the coming changes. Rather than resist what was happening, he actually volunteered to help move the program along. The result was that Sam was given a bigger job with more responsibilities in his area of expertise. Had he not paid attention to the shift in the company's philosophy, Sam more than likely would today be unemployed.

91. A New Direction Can Change the Culture

The flip side of company culture is all hard-boiled business. When business is bad, you can bet change is coming and with it, a tidal wave of culture shifts. When a business goes into survivor mode, the old rules—written and unwritten—get tossed overboard. The easygoing days of admiring the poetry of the mission/vision statement are in the past. You would be well served to be living every word. Keeping your job means figuring out how you can apply the principles of the mission/vision statement to what is happening, where it is happening, and how it is going to affect the company.

During downsizing, political activity steps up. People try to solidify their support networks and connections to influence. You should be doing the same. Touch base with your support group—peers, manager—but also look for the people who are influencing management and leading the change. Once you identify those people, try to get connected to them. Above all, you want to demonstrate to the influence leaders that you have a positive attitude and want to contribute in a positive way.

Don't be surprised to find your manager leaning heavily on people to bring them in line with the new business and cultural reality. The days when you went along to get along with your colleagues are gone. It's every one for him- or herself. The department culture that said people can come in late, take a long lunch, or leave early no longer applies. If you're interested in saving your job, forget that you ever considered that behavior acceptable, which, by the way, you should never have.

Your manager will reward you only if you make the change. And just as certainly, management will punish you if you don't. So, from a cultural standpoint, you want to publicly demonstrate the behavior that closely aligns with what your manager wants, and that leads in the direction the company is moving. Do anything else, even if that means lying low until things blow over, and you will be targeted for termination. You either get with the program or get ready to leave.

Scan the horizon. Look for islands of stability and strength inside the company. If there is a department whose work is important to the organization's future, make a connection and try to move your job to that group.

When change hit Mark's company, his small web design department at an insurance company suddenly became very popular. Why? The company decided to slowly phase out most of its printing jobs in favor of expanding its presence on the web. The major cultural change not only sent ripples through the company but made Mark's group the focal point of the company's future. Reacting to the cultural shift, people began calling, e-mailing, and knocking on Mark's door looking for a job. Employees understood that if they wanted to keep their jobs, they had to make connections in Mark's department and begin acquiring the necessary skills that would allow them to transfer into the organization that was going to lead the company into the future.

92. Be Self-Assured but Not Arrogant

Businesses keep self-assured employees—if they are not arrogant jackasses. The best self-assured employees tend to be low-maintenance because they are self-starters with positive, can-do attitudes. Of course, some self-assured employees don't understand the nuanced difference between confidence and arrogance (see Tip 4). In large measure, it comes down to how you interact with colleagues.

Take the case of Charles, a highly competent, uniquely qualified businessman. His competency and excellent qualifications made him someone who was in considerable demand. Of course, those qualities also contributed to him being an absolute arrogant, intolerable ass. Charles's employer tolerated him because he was an expert in his field and a money magnet. But nobody, not his manager, his manager's managers, and certainly not his employees, liked Charles even a little bit.

But that didn't matter to him. He was too busy routinely belittling the people who worked under him. He micromanaged their every move, and heaven forbid if they didn't write a report his way. Charles's employees were so afraid of having his wrath turned on them, that no one ever challenged him. Not that he would have heard it. He was usually too busy stroking his own ego by telling anyone who would listen about his many accomplishments.

But Charles made money for the company, lots of money. And over a decade or so he advanced through the ranks to the point where he was almost untouchable. But then some equally as talented, and certainly less arrogant, golden-haired boys and girls joined the company. Charles was suddenly no longer the only genius in the organization. But what really snapped him to attention was when the CEO ordered all her senior managers to participate in a 360 performance evaluation, where people from every level assess your job performance.

The feedback stunned him. Finding out that no one liked him, with lists of the reasons why they didn't like him, and everyone having the same reasons on their lists, was like a shot of 100-proof reality. Charles was told to change his management style or be fired. He wasn't so arrogant anymore.

Even for a manager and a top producer, being an arrogant employee is a dead-end road. Don't confuse self-assurance with arrogance. It won't win you friends but it will make you expendable. If you have in the past confused being self-assured with being arrogant, you will have some fences to mend. Start by doing an honest, in-depth self-assessment. Then figure out ways you can correct your attitude. Humility is very important in rehabilitating your image. But you must be authentic. Your manager will see through insincerity like he is looking through glass. He will be looking for consistency over an extended period of time. But making the transition will help you save your job, and maybe even make you a few new friends.

WHO WOULD YOU CHOOSE?

Two highly capable employees with the same talents and skills join a company. The first employee is assigned to a team that has been working on a project. The new person comes in and immediately starts criticizing the work already done by the team members. The new person then goes on to insist that his way would be better.

The second new employee is assigned to another team, which has also been working on a project. The new person asks about the project's goals and objectives, what the team is currently working on, and how she can be of help.

Which of those two people would you rather work with?

93. When to Be Guarded Giving Your First Impression

Deciding when and when not to voice your gut reaction to your manager can be dicey, especially when you are concerned about keeping your job. But the real chainsaw juggling starts when your manager's manager asks for your immediate reaction to an issue.

The one thing you can't do is walk away. Nor can you deflect an answer by saying something like "This is a complex issue, and I need additional facts. I'll get back to you tomorrow." Sorry, Charlie, but that answer just moved you to the head of the soon-to-be-unemployed line.

When your manager's manager asks for your gut reaction, you have to think on your feet—quickly. The key is to start thinking before you enter the meeting room by:

✔ Getting the agenda and doing research
✔ Finding out who is presenting what issues
✔ Asking people what they think is coming out of the meeting
✔ Asking your boss what she thinks is brewing
✔ Listening intently to the presentations and discussion
✔ Thinking about what you heard in the context of your manager, department, or group

Then, when you see the big exec coming your way, you are ready. Try to quickly judge the intent of her question. Is the executive trying to lure you into saying something that can later be used against your manager? If that is the case, respond as objectively and obliquely as possible. Do not contradict your manager's position, and stick to the facts without indicating whether or not you agree with your boss.

As soon as the encounter ends, high-tail it over to your manager and tell him what happened, and exactly what you said. Even if you said the wrong thing, tell your boss. You don't want your manager thinking that you threw him under the bus. Your manager should understand that you had no choice but to give your gut reaction and may have misspoken. Plus, by telling him what happened, you are reinforcing your support for them. It all adds up to the manager giving you points that will help you keep your job.

But it's not over yet. What if after the meeting, your manager's manager comes to you and says, "Charlie, I'd like your gut reaction about the way your manager handled this situation. Oh, and this is strictly off the record between the two of us." That sick feeling in your stomach has nothing to do with your gut reaction. It's your career flashing before your eyes. Welcome to a no-win situation. So what can you do?

Read the situation, and then have the courage to make a judgment call. You don't want to endanger in any way the people you are supporting. At the same time, you don't want to anger someone powerful if you can at all help it. In any case, do what is ethical and right. Tell the senior executive that you would like to help but that you feel that it is inappropriate to respond to her question. Then suggest that she discuss the issue directly with your manager.

Without knowing it, you may have passed a test. Your manager's manager may have been testing to see if, under pressure, you would sell out your boss. If you work for good people, being ethical should earn you enough points to keep your job for as long as you want it.

THE IRONY OF IT ALL

After you give your manager's manager your gut reaction, you do the right thing and immediately tell your boss. You are off the hook, and your job is safe, right? Not necessarily. It all depends what your manager decides to do with the information you fed him. If your supervisor is a jerk, he may take your intelligence and use it against someone else. If it is traced back to you—and it will be—you may find yourself in trouble with a much higher authority.

94. Inspect and Maintain Your Bridges

One key to keeping your job in a bad economic environment is how well you inspect and maintain your business bridges. Unless you possess some extraordinarily rare technical prowess, or are otherwise uniquely talented, you need other people.

Those people are your business bridges. They may or may not be part of your network. But they are people who are connected to either your company or industry and know a lot of other folks. So the first rule of business bridges is, never burn one. That said, almost everyone, at some time in their career, has gleefully ignited a business bridge. It usually occurs early in their career, and, at the time, it probably felt great telling the person that they were a doofus.

Don't do it again. You never know when, where, or why your name comes up in a conversation and your old boss is telling everyone that you're a self-important moron. Technology has shrunk the business world, and word travels fast. No matter how much of a jerk you think someone is, regardless of how justified you feel about releasing a full volley of your wrath on them, hold your tongue. When the impulse to unload on someone strikes you, remember Tip Number 41: Be Civil to Your Colleagues. You don't have to like your colleague or boss. You don't have to pal around with them. But you must treat them politely and courteously. It just makes good business sense and it's one more bridge left intact.

Now that your bridges are fireproofed, you have to conscientiously inspect and maintain each one. Maintaining good relationships, after all, requires work. You especially want to cultivate and nurture a core group of people to be your trusted allies and supporters. But choose those people wisely. Don't select people based solely on practical, utilitarian reasons. You should like and respect the people in your core group because a big part of maintaining your relationships means talking to them fairly often. You are going to hear about their jobs, their families, and their weekend plans. That can become tedious when you don't like someone. More importantly, if you do choose people for self-serving reasons, you will be seen as callous, cynical, and calculating, and subvert your brand.

Nevertheless, you want your core group to be people ascending in power. It doesn't help to have someone on a downward trajectory watching your back. You need people influential in the organization so that when layoffs are discussed they will represent you. Identify people who wield influence in the organization, and, to the extent you can, align yourself with them. It could be your boss, or her boss, or someone to whom you have no natural connection.

Since relationships are two-way streets, part of maintaining and inspecting your bridges is helping your business supporter advance his agenda in any way you can. Find out what is important to each core member and then what you can do to contribute to their success. Look for opportunities to work together and offer solid, relevant, and timely advice and information.

THE NEXT GENERATION

When trying to configure your inner circle of allies and supporters, don't forget the Next Generation; you know, the rising stars who haven't yet quite hit the big time.

"You have to look for individuals that matter in the organization, who are going places, who have an impact and are seen as influential," says Jim Allen, vice president of Booz Allen Hamilton, a management consulting firm located in McLean, Virginia. "You can either pay attention to them and cultivate a relationship, or you can be oblivious to them and hope for the best."

95. Edit Your E-Mail

E-mail is the twenty-first-century version of the office memo. But unlike the paper memo, which had to be physically handled and edited after it was typed, the electronic version is instantly dispatched with the push of a button. And therein lies the problem.

Most people become defensive when they receive an e-mail critical of them; this is an understandable human reaction. Really now, who among us enjoys being corrected or scolded? But too often that defensiveness transforms into anger on the screen in the form of a response. And then, click, the button is pushed, and an emotionally charged, highly inflammable, for-every-action-there-is-a-reaction response is wending its way back to the sender.

E-mail helps you keep your job by learning to use it judiciously. Look, it's a given that you are going to receive your share of blood-pressure-raising e-mails. So be ready not to respond by having a strategy in place. For instance, instead of instantaneously sending your snarky retort, save the e-mail in your draft file. When you cool down, read it again. Still want to send it? Okay, but first apply this rule of thumb: Would you say everything in your e-mail to the person if he were standing in front of you? Everyone develops byte bravado and virtual muscles when he or she doesn't have to stare directly into the other person's eyes. You know that the chances of a confrontation are almost nil if you're in one division of the company several floors or miles away from your nemesis.

But if you still feel justified in unloading on your e-mail adversary and he is just floors away, get out of your chair and walk over to see him—face to face. Sure, you're still going to tell him what you think. But even money says that your argument will likely be much less profane, and presented in a much more professional manner.

If your foe is too far away, pick up the telephone. There are so many advantages to using the phone over e-mail. For one, it is real-time dialogue, which means any misunderstanding can be instantly corrected. In addition, you hear the person's tone, their attitude, and you can probe his or her reasoning.

Since e-mail is commonly used for internal communications among employees, you should be careful about the conversations you join, or are included in. Every e-mail message leaves an electronic trail. You don't want to be involved in any e-mail exchanges that complain about a company policy or practice, or criticize and make fun of a boss. All are grounds for dismissal, even if you do not add a comment. You will be viewed as being complicit, the classic guilty by association.

Take the case of Larry, who played on his company's ice hockey team. Like all the players, Larry was part of the team's internal e-mail group, which received a weekly list of game times and locations. One week, however, Larry found more than just a game schedule when he opened his e-mail. Squeezed between the next opponent and rink location was a rant by the team captain, going off on his boss, calling him a loser and more. In no time, Larry's inbox was filled with replies from other teammates chiming in with gripes about their managers.

Larry didn't respond or make any comment about his manager. Still, he felt uneasy about the exchanges. So he did exactly what you should do if you find yourself in a similar situation. First, he called a couple of his teammates and told them that, not only was the e-mail unprofessional, but dangerous for them to use the company's e-mail to complain about their managers. Then he went online and replied to the last e-mail, asking that he not be included on the mailing list for anything other than game times and locations.

96. Develop Organizational Awareness

If you want to keep your job, you must understand the internal workings of your company. That skill is called organizational awareness and means knowing how things get accomplished by understanding how your department's work fits into the company's overall system. For instance, if you work in accounting, processing invoices of sales receipts, you recognize how your work connects to what the salespeople do for a living.

Organizational awareness helps you keep your job by teaching you how to get things done beyond the boundaries of your department. Knowing the way relationships work between and among different departments is an invaluable piece of business information. With that knowledge comes the realization that titles sometimes don't matter. When it comes to getting things done, what matters is who has the influence. You need to identify and build relationships with people who will be helpful and supportive, as well as show you where the resources you need are located, if you want to be successful.

For instance, if you are not organizationally aware, you may try to bypass people and go right to the top to pitch your project or idea. That simply isn't a smart thing to do. First of all, a top executive is usually too busy to hear your pitch, and likely will be more annoyed with you than interested in your idea. But more to the point, if the big boss rejects your concept, the project is dead. Why? You have already gone to the top. There is no higher court of appeals.

Now, if you are organizationally aware, you would take a different path that would start with finding out who wields real influence in the organization. That person may not have a fancy title or an important job, but, for whatever reason, he has a good relationship with the boss. That person will know the type of projects the executive is interested in. He will know if today is a good or bad day to submit your proposal. If he likes your project, it has a really good shot of getting on the CEO's agenda.

Organizational awareness is also connected to your company's mission/vision statement. In this situation it means that you understand the company's values, its business principles, the company's code of conduct, and the image the organization wants to project. If you are organizationally aware, you reflect those values to the outside world.

A good example is Federal Express, which is renowned for being customer-service oriented and having employees who really live the company's mission statement. A business colleague recently went to Federal Express for a business meeting. He entered the lobby and went directly to the receptionist and announced his appointment. The receptionist got up from her chair, came around the desk, extended her hand, and welcomed him to Federal Express. The man was floored. In all his business travels it was the first and only time a receptionist had so completely represented the corporation's values. And to his delight, he received the same greeting from everyone he met that day at Federal Express.

By being organizationally aware, you can have the same impact inside your company. If you are in accounting, why not take a stroll over to the sales department and introduce yourself? Explain that you are the guy handling the receipts the department sends over. Take the extra step and ask if there is anything you can do to make the salesperson's job easier. That simple gesture of reaching across boundaries will have a tremendous effect on people. Your manager will recognize that you know how to make connections and get things done. And that makes you someone he wants to keep around.

97. Learn the Importance of Knowing How to Influence People

Influencing is a basic, natural skill. You may not realize it, but every day you influence the people around you. You may want them do something for you, or to give you something you want.

When it comes to business, however, influencing requires more strategy and sophistication. So, if you are good at influencing people in business, it can help save your job. If you are good at influencing people, your manager will not only respect and value you as an employee but view you as someone who knows how to navigate the company's political system.

There are some basic principles to mastering the art of influence. To successfully influence someone, you must work behind the scenes to build a base of support, because it is difficult to influence alone. The late business consultant Joel DeLuca created the 51 percent rule of influencing. The rule states that, before you present an idea, you must know that 51 percent of the people in the room support it.

Let's say you want to influence your manager about a project, or you need extra funding. Long before the meeting, start talking to your colleagues about your idea. You want them to be familiar with, and excited about, your proposal. If you spring your idea on people for the first time at the meeting, you are catching them cold. Chances are everyone in the room—say fewer than 51 percent—won't respond positively to your idea. Therefore, before you try to influence at the meeting, lobby your coworkers ahead of time. You will need that base of support if you expect to be successful.

You also want to seek support from people in your organization already known as great influencers. Prior to the meeting, find the people who have the manager's ear, and try to get them to agree to support your idea.

But you still are not ready to enter your manager's office. No matter how much you have rehearsed and prepared, do more homework. Before you walk into the meeting, try to anticipate how he is going to respond to your influencing attempt. Ask your colleagues how they think your manager will respond. Try to project any questions your manager might have, and be ready to counter any objections.

If you can show your manager your ability to influence other people, then you will be considered a valued employee. And valued employees don't lose their jobs.

98. Influence People Through Conversation

As you become more familiar and skillful at influencing people, you learn ways of convincing people to support your agenda. Still, the single most important way to influence someone is by engaging him or her in active conversation.

Active conversation occurs when you encourage, invite, and respect another person's point of view during your discussion. In fact, you want the person to talk freely, because the more he or she reveals about any objections to your idea, the more information you have to use in gaining that person's support. But you must listen to what he or she is saying to make sure that you also hear what you agree about. When you identify those areas, repeat or paraphrase them as a way of confirming what you have heard, and to remind the individual that you share common ground.

To gather even more ammunition, ask the person leading and open-ended questions. You want to smoke out the point where you disagree. Once you have that information, you can begin building an argument to counter those objections. Being influential in a conversation is all about listening for areas of agreement, and encouraging honest talk about disagreements or different points of view.

Another way to try to influence someone is by appealing to his or her self interests. For example, if you want your manager to change the way work is distributed in your department, consider how changing the work system can make him look good. Now, when presenting your work redistribution plan, add that your method would save a position. Saving a position—and the money that goes along with it—will make your manager look good with the executives.

You also may know that your manager is a bit of an egotist. Use that information to get what you want. How? By making your idea his idea. Say something like, "I know that you have been putting a lot of energy into cutting costs, Sam. Well, following your lead, this thought came to me." When you leave the meeting, your manager will know that you are deferring to him. But that little tactic probably will influence your manager enough to get the work distribution changed.

Another method of influencing is an all-out blitz of doing as many connected things as possible. So, if you want to influence your manager to change the distribution of work, research data on a plan similar to yours. Then, if another department in the company has already implemented a new work distribution plan, ask for the information and forward it to your manager, including how much money was saved. Go outside the company to find organizations like yours that are trying new work schemes. Give all the information to your manager. He may not even look at it. But the fact that you have reports on work distribution plans from both inside and outside your organization adds to the credibility of your idea. In turn, that increases your influence with your manager.

KNOW WHEN TO INFLUENCE

Before you attempt to influence anyone, make sure he or she is in the proper frame of mind. On a particular day, your manager may have too many other pressing issues to listen to you. Don't force the issue. Gauge your manager's receptiveness to what you want to do. If she isn't ready, don't submit your idea. Instead, listen to what she wants to talk about and save your idea for

another day. Influencing people is all about knowing
when to show your cards and when to hold them.

99. Don't Spread Rumors

Business rumors get started when people in an organization
aren't given all the facts about an issue. So you might say that
most rumors aren't started to instigate problems, but to fill information gaps.

In business there is real truth—the facts and logic—and
political truth—the spin the organization, manager, or employee
applies to an issue to accommodate an agenda. Political truth is
the organization's attempt to control how people react to what is
happening inside the company. Managers and executives know
that a group of people reading the same information will likely
arrive at very different interpretations of the data. A good example is the stock market. It doesn't matter if it goes up 500 points,
or down 500 points, you will find plenty of people ready to
explain the reason in several different ways. Why? Because people simply apply their own meaning to the numbers.

When a company is hit by hard times, people want all the up-to-
the-minute information they can get. Employees worried about their
jobs want to know what the executives know, from what they are
thinking to plans that are in the works. Senior management, con-
versely, wants to control the release of as much information as possible, as well as how it is interpreted. The gap between what is known
and what is being withheld is filled by the assumptions, beliefs, and
imaginations of individuals. And that is how rumors are born.

Employees, however, don't consider their elucidation as
rumor mongering, because it echoes what they believe. So, how
can you use rumors to help you save your job? Essentially by
debunking each one as it flies fast and furious around you. Look,

when it comes to rumors, you can either join in and add a little something of your own to the story, or you can take the high road and stay above the fray. The choice is yours. But if you want to keep your job, be the better person and don't gossip. Instead, help your company, manager, and coworkers by searching out more facts that will bring you closer to the truth, which you can then use to counter and correct the rumor.

The best place to stomp out a rumor is at a department or team meeting. When the topic comes up—and it will—you can interject how you have done more research and discovered information that mitigates or otherwise debunks the rumor. Your manager will see you as a helpful, trustworthy employee and thank you for standing up for the best interests of the company.

On the other hand, some of your colleagues may see you as a turncoat for not joining the "ain't it awful the way the company is treating us" bandwagon. That will officially put you on the outside with your coworkers. Don't sweat it. Any time you make a decision about a complex issue it almost always will create another dilemma. And really, the decision to shoot down a rumor isn't that difficult. All you have to do is decide what you should do and how you should act if you want to keep your job. When you think of it like that, the logical path is pretty clearly defined.

You can ease the tensions by circling back after the meeting and doing some fence mending with your coworkers. Explain your position and try to show your colleagues that what you did was in their best interest. Say something like, "It doesn't help us to continue playing into the rumor because it makes us look like we are part of the problem."

If one or two of your coworkers reject your explanation and still think that you sold out to management, do you really want to be identified with the group that management views as part of the problem? Don't worry about them. If they continue thinking the same way, they won't be around for long.

100. Have a Speech to Counter Negative Comments

When times are bad at work, it's hard to avoid running into a colleague who isn't down and griping about the company. You should be prepared to parry that thrust with a strong, positive elevator speech.

Why is it called an elevator speech? Because, traditionally, in the elevator is where people have a few free moments to chat with colleagues. It could just as easily be called a vending-machine speech, or getting-a-cup-of-coffee speech.

Your elevator speech stops you from being swamped by the rising tide of negativity. It should show people that your brand is steady and even-keeled, yet realistic.

Anyway, back to the elevator. You push the button, and as the doors open, Fred from marketing walks up. Being sociable, you ask Fred how things are going. Normally, it is a perfectly polite, nonincendiary question. But not in troubled times. Before you know it, old Fred is telling you just how awful this quarter's numbers are, what lunkheads the bosses are, how layoff rumors are keeping him up at night, and that the new hand soap in the men's washroom makes his hands dry.

What do you say to avoid being drenched by Fred's thunder-cloud of despair? People facing a serious disruption in their lives need affirmation. So, whatever you do, don't be dismissive. Show some sympathy. Acknowledge that things aren't great right now, then immediately roll out your prepared, upbeat elevator speech. Tell Fred that, while there is reason for concern, these challenges bring out the best in people. Explain that you are staying focused and doing what you can to move the company forward, and how that perspective keeps you mentally in the game and your job performance at a high level. You might even suggest that Fred give that kind of can-do attitude a test drive.

The secret to really selling your elevator speech is believing every word. If you don't, Fred and all your colleagues will see through your spiel and lose respect for you and your brand. So explain to yourself why you believe good can come from the company's current situation, and how it can be accomplished. Then write it out and practice it before you present it.

101. Take Control of Your Career

There is just this one last tip, and that is, no one but you can make your life and career a success. We can give you 101 tips about ways that will help you save your job. But in the end, it is you who must supply the energy, the ideas, the hard work, and the determination. When confronted with a wall blocking you from your goal, it is you who must figure out a way to scramble over the top or burrow underneath so you can continue on your quest.

Realize that the goal of this book is not for you to use all 101 tips. Instead, look at the tips as a set of interconnecting ideas and methods. It is up to you, the reader, to determine which of these tips work for you, considering your circumstances. And yes, it will be different for each person. So we suggest that one approach to getting the most from this book is to reread the five, ten, or twenty-five tips that resonate with you and seem to offer the most viable approach for you. Look at those tips, and see if there is a pattern that proposes a particular path. Perhaps you are drawn to tips like taking issues off your manager's plate, taking on more assignments, and learning new skills. Those three would seem to indicate that you need to educate yourself about how the company and your department operate, so that you know how things get done.

Now, consider which one of those items seems the most important to your manager, and you have the beginnings of a plan that will see you taking on more focused assignments, becoming a better team player, and adding value to your department. You might want to start writing down ideas and flesh out a plan, including the specific strategies you want to employ that will enhance your status and importance to your department and manager.

Allow us one last suggestion, and that is to find a mentor or create a board of advisers as soon as possible. Remember, you want people who will support and help you and talk you through your plans, while offering their ideas and guidance.

Finally, remember, this book was written as a guide, not an answer sheet. The only way to get answers is for you to get involved in developing your career. But be forewarned that if you choose to take no action, your job is vulnerable. You have to take charge of your career. You do control your own destiny. All it takes to get results and save your job is a dedicated, honest effort from you.

Index

About the Authors

Michael J. Kitson, MBA has spent thirty-five years as a business consultant. He has worked at all organizational levels including as a consultant to front-line management, department heads, and organized labor. He is experienced in strategic human-resource development and has worked with a number of industries, including insurance, banking, industrial and consumer products, telecommunications, and health care. He is currently principal of Michael Kitson Associates.

Bob Calandra has been writing professionally for more than thirty years. His award-winning work has appeared in national and regional consumer magazines, trade magazines, and newspapers. The former editor of a regional business magazine, he has written, coauthored, and ghosted four books, including *A History of Pediatric Otolaryngology at The Children's Hospital of Philadelphia,* and *Noble Intent,* a business management philosophy for the twenty-first century.